AF352293

A Story
of
Intrigue
Passion
Violence
and Death

James Veitch

The First Narrative Gospel
of the
New Testament

By convention called and known as
The Gospel of Saint Mark

A modern translation with an introduction
and afterword

by

James Veitch

For ease of reading, the following format has been used:

- All speech is shown in *italics*.

- Jesus' speech is accentuated by being indented from the left-hand margin.

- Teaching sections in the gospels are indented on both left and right margins.

- Quotes are indented on both margins and in **bold** print. Quotes within teaching sections are therefore indented twice from both margins.

- For emphasis, **bold** type is also used.

ISBN: 0-908815-37-9

© 1994 James Veitch. All rights reserved. No part of this publication may be reproduced, stored or transmitted in any form or by any means without the prior written permission of the publisher.

Colcom Press
6 Albert Hall Drive, Red Beach,
Hibiscus Coast, Aotearoa-New Zealand

Desktop publishing: Lesley Fischer

For the Congregation of
St Anselm's Union Church
Karori, Wellington

Preface

A number of friends have read this translation and made many suggestions. Most of these I have been glad to incorporate.

My translation of *Mark* is part of Volume Two of my New Testament in a modern translation, arranged in chronological order, published under the title: *Searching for Identity and Founding the Church.*

I believe Mark was meant to be read and listened to at a single sitting and I therefore present it on its own and in this form in the hope it might be used in this way.

The Afterword and Bibliography on *Mark* has been added especially for this publication.

My thanks to Lesley Fischer for her patience in producing draft after draft of the translation.

Some members of the congregation at St Anselm's Union Church read this narrative gospel in the way I believe was intended by its creator at an evening service on Passion Sunday in the liturgical year of Mark, 1994. I thank them and the members of the congregation for this occasion and for their support.

James Veitch
Passion Sunday
27 March 1994.

Introduction

According to a suggestion made by Bishop Papias of Hierapolis (60–140CE) which is reported by Eusebius (260–339CE), this gospel was written by John Mark, a friend of Paul and of Peter. Papias quotes a person named presbyter, or elder John, who passed on the information that Mark wrote this gospel from conversations he had had with Peter—hence the frequency with which Peter is mentioned in the gospel.

The connection between Mark and this gospel certainly seems to have been widely accepted in the early Christian community.

It is said John Mark was with Peter in Rome and took notes from the conversations they had. Then later when he lived in Alexandria in upper Egypt the notes were revised and re-edited to produce what is known to us as the Gospel of Mark.

However a close reading of this gospel raises questions about the traditional link.

It seems to have circulated some time after the upheavals of 64CE in Rome and after the Jewish-Roman war of 66-70 in Israel/Palestine had come to an end. I think it is possible that it circulated at the time Masada fell to the Romans in 73-74, some forty-five years after the execution of Jesus.

In standard translations of the New Testament, Mark chapter 13 stands out because of its use of unusual language and ideas. In the background there are obviously traumatic events which have recently taken place and which have shaped the thinking of those who created this picture of the end of the world.

But this is not all. The content of the gospel reflects the social, economic and political situation of the Galilee and Jerusalem of an earlier time—thus suggesting the material used in the preparation of the gospel was collected over a number of years.

I imagine this gospel is made up from edited versions or summaries of sermons given and discussed in the communities of faith.

These sermons would have been given by itinerant preachers or visiting missionaries who made use of incidents in the life of Jesus, parables and other forms of teaching connected with him, as well as words attributed to him.

These sermons would have been discussed by community members and then related to their Jewish background, if that was appropriate and relevant, and to their religious and philosophical setting in the part of the Greco-Roman world where they lived.

If there were no itinerant preachers or missionaries available, I imagine the communities would have had a collection of incidents, stories and sayings to discuss. There were pastors and teachers to assist in these discussions.

Over the years each community would have built up its own understanding of who they believed Jesus to be. How they came to think about faith in God would have developed out of such a context.

The creative imagination of both preacher and listener is thus crucial for the way in which the incidents, stories and words were told, retold, remembered, and eventually written down. Until written collections of the sayings of Jesus appeared and began circulation, the situation would have been fluid if not chaotic (Kelber, 1983, p31).

Written gospels thus came into existence to impose order on chaos and to standardise the traditions about Jesus. Once written gospels appeared, the oral traditions were of less value, for written words have greater authority than spoken words.

If theories explaining the existence of the *Secret Gospel of Mark* have any merit, then it is to remind us that this gospel circulated in at least three editions before the appearance of the version we now know.

According to Clement of Alexandria, there was firstly the public Gospel of Mark, used in the instruction of converts prior to their becoming members of the communities of faith by baptism.

Secondly, there was the Secret Gospel, used by those who wanted to grow more deeply in their knowledge of the faith.

Thirdly, there was the Carpocration version of the Gospel of Mark, an amplification of the Secret Gospel which was eventually rejected by the Christian community and disappeared.

Finally, there is what is known to us as the First Narrative Gospel or Canonical Mark (Crossan: 1992, p61ff; see also Koester 1983; Smith 1973). Once this canonical version circulated and became established, the public and secret gospel versions fell into disuse and eventually disappeared.

There never was an original message which the apostles and early Christians were committed to preserving and handing on (Kelber 1983). The narrative gospel evolved, coming into existence to meet a need for a standardised version for the life of Jesus which could be used with confidence in the communities of faith which had sprung into existence in the fifties, sixties and seventies.

I have called this gospel a *narrative gospel* to call attention to its literary form as a story (Crossan, 1988).

We usually encounter Mark in a piecemeal fashion as portions of it are read in a church service, but it is a complete story:

> *Although the author of the Gospel of Mark certainly used sources rooted in the historical events surrounding the life of Jesus, the final text is a literary creation with an autonomous integrity. . .One can read and interpret Mark's Gospel as a story independent from the real people and events upon which it is based. The author. . .has not simply collected traditions, organised them, made connections between them, and added summaries but has also told a story—a dramatic story—*(Rhoads and Mechie, 1982 p3).

I will take a step further than this and suggest that the story *Mark* unfolds, does not have to be *rooted in historical events surrounding the life of Jesus* but has an integrity of its own as it presents Jesus as the human face of God.

This is a highly creative presentation which appeals strongly to the issues and questions faced by humans in every decade of world history. It is presented out of a particular human situation, for humans struggling to be human and keep their faith in God in similar situations.

In this respect it is very different from the *Book of Q* and initiates a risky, innovative departure in the presentation of the life of Jesus. (I will write about this later in the companion volume to this translation).

The particular stance taken in this gospel is this: *Jesus is the human face of God and this discovery has major implications for the way society is structured, organised and run, particularly on a social, economic and religious level* (see for example Myers, 1991).

If God is present in the life and death of Jesus in the way *Mark* presents, then there will be a major difference in the way people live and in the way the world is run.

This is the good news, **God is present in the life of Jesus of Galilee (Jesus of Nazareth).**

The followers of Jesus are called upon to change the way they live, to challenge the existing situation in the world and to inject new forces of change so that God has a voice in the world.

Reference in the gospel is made to a mysterious figure written about in the **Book of Daniel**, which is found in the Hebrew Bible. The words which require our attention are found in Daniel 7: 13ff:

> *During this vision which I had during the night, I saw what appeared to be a human being. He approached me, surrounded by clouds, and he went to the one who had been living forever and was introduced to him. He was given authority, honour, royal position and dignity so that all the peoples of the world, from every nation, race and speaking every language known, would serve him. He will exercise this authority forever and the community he founds and directs will exist for all time!*

It is my contention that the creators of the Gospel of Mark believed that Jesus was this figure.

In other translations, this figure is, for the most part, called *the son of man*. I have chosen to identify Jesus with this son of man, believing that was the intention of the creators of the gospel.

When Jesus talks in this way, identifying himself with this figure from the **Book of Daniel**, he makes connections and causes deep concern amongst his close friends and this is reflected in my translation.

For the creators of this gospel, Jesus **is** the figure who has come and inaugurated a new period in the history of the world. He will come again at the end of time as the judge of all the people who have ever lived in the life of this planet. Jesus, in this respect, is God's right hand.

To get the full impact of this gospel, it's better to read it as a whole. I have divided it very artificially into four sections, just to give some orientation to the reader. These headings, however, should be ignored. They are not part of the original text.

Originally the gospel was meant to be read without chapter breaks or headings and to be listened to.

The words create a picture and the picture is very powerful. It is designed to change the hearers' thinking and to call them into living a different lifestyle. It is story-telling at its very best.

The Prelude

This story is an account of the good news about God present in our world through the life and death of Jesus.

It all began just as God said it would in these words written by Isaiah:

I am sending my messenger
to prepare the way ahead;
In the semi desert someone is shouting—
Get the road ready!   God is coming!
Straighten out the road and level it!
God is nearly here! (40: 3).

John was this messenger, and appeared out of the semi desert saying to all who cared to listen:

If you are serious about a change of heart
turn your lives over to God!
Take a ritual bath here in the Jordan river
if you are sincere!
Then and only then will all your wrongdoing
be overlooked and forgotten by God!

Many ordinary people hearing about John's activities went to see first-hand what he was doing and to listen to him.   They came from Jerusalem and its surrounding area.

As soon as they recognised their wrongdoing and said they were sorry for ignoring God's claim upon their lives, John supervised a ritual bath for them in the Jordan river.

John was an unusual person!   His clothes made from camels' skins were fastened around his waist by a leather belt.   He ate grasshoppers and wild honey.

In the course of what he said to the people were these words which he often repeated:

Someone much more significant than me
is about to come amongst us!
When that day dawns and the person arrives,
no-one, including me,
will have the right to kneel down
and untie his sandal fastenings and welcome him.
I supervise your ritual cleansing,
but this person will help you experience
the presence of God in your lives!

Not long afterwards Jesus came down from the town of Nazareth in Galilee and was making his way towards Jerusalem when he heard about John.

He stopped off, listened, and was persuaded by what he heard.

He was immersed in the Jordan river by John, to show that he was committing his life to God and as a sign that he was starting a new life.

Jesus said later this event was the turning point of his life.

As he came up from beneath the water, he saw the sky open above him, and he felt the presence of God vividly alive within him when he saw a dove fly down and rest on his shoulder.   He heard a voice say with authority:

You are my own son,
the apple of my eye!
my kindness, compassion and love
will flow through your life!

Almost immediately Jesus found himself alone in a forbidding landscape, high above the Jordan river where John was working.   He spent a considerable time there.   The only signs of life he saw were wild animals. But God took good care of him as he faced up to the significance of this turning point in his life, and the implications on it of the vivid experience he had felt of God's presence.

Jesus in Galilee

Later still after he had heard of John's arrest, Jesus moved to the Jewish villages and towns of the Galilee talking to people about God.

What he said can be summarised in these words:

Your time is up!
You are about to experience the presence of God in a new way!
Don't leave God out of your lives!
Take God seriously!

One day Jesus was making his way along a path that skirted the sea of Galilee when he stopped to watch the brothers, Simon and Andrew, fishing not far from the shore.

Jesus called out to the brothers:

Come with me!

I will show you how to really hook fish! (Jeremiah 16:16).

The two were so impressed with Jesus they gave up fishing and followed him.

Further along the seaside the group came across James and John, the sons of Zebedee, who were sitting in their boat mending nets.

Come with me! Jesus said to them—and they did!

Before leaving, they made arrangements for daily workers to be taken on in their places.

Jesus and his friends made their base in Capernaum.

On the first sacred day (called the Sabbath by Jews) they strode into the Jewish place of meeting (the synagogue) where worship and other activities are held.

During the course of the service Jesus was asked to comment on the reading for that day from the Hebrew Bible.

When he had finished everyone was amazed at his insight.   The way he explained the meaning of the passage left a deep impression on them.   His style was very different from the scholars they were used to hearing.

Without warning a person, known to be mentally disturbed, rushed into the synagogue screaming:

Hey you from Nazareth!

Why are you here?

We have nothing in common!

Have you come to get rid of us—kill us all off?

I know who you really are—you are God's holy one!

Jesus was not affected by this outburst:

Shut up!   Leave this person alone! he shouted.

The person shook all over, screamed and was silent.

There was pandemonium in the synagogue.   Everyone began to talk at once:

What's going on?

This is surely different!

Is this new teaching?

What kind of a person is it who does this sort of thing?

Even evil spirits do what he says!

As soon as the service was over reports of what had happened spread rapidly throughout Capernaum and the surrounding villages.

Jesus went to the house of Simon and Andrew which was nearby.   James and John were with him.   There, Jesus heard Simon's mother-in-law was in bed with a high temperature.

He went straight to the bedside, took her hand in his and helped her up. The fever abated.   She then felt well enough to make them all a meal.

As soon as the sacred day was over, the whole of Capernaum gathered outside the door bringing with them their sick and mentally disturbed. Jesus healed many. Those possessed by evil spirits knew his real identity but he would not let them reveal it.

As dawn broke the next morning, Jesus got up and went outside the town to a place where he could pray undisturbed on his own. The others, finding he had gone, started searching for him.

When they found him they said:

Everyone in the town wants to meet with you!

Jesus replied:

> *Let's move on to nearby towns and villages. I want to tell others about God. This is what I feel called to do.*

Jesus and his friends then moved around the Galilee, speaking in synagogues and healing people, particularly the mentally disturbed.

On one occasion, a man with a horrifying skin disease which kept him in isolation from his family, friends and the rest of his hometown approached Jesus. Falling on his knees he pleaded:

You can make me well if you really want to!

Jesus replied:

> *Yes I want to. You are well!*

Immediately the skin disease disappeared and the man was healed.

Jesus then talked seriously with the man:

> *Don't go around telling everyone about what I have done. Go straight to the priests in the temple at Jerusalem and show them you are well; take part in the ceremony set out in the rules and regulations we were given in ancient times (Leviticus 14); then everyone will know you are well again.*

But the man was so happy he told everyone what Jesus had done and this set people talking about him and clamouring for attention. He was no longer free to go where he planned and tried to keep out of people's way, but as soon as he was known to be in an area people came to him.

When Jesus returned to Capernaum a few days later word spread he was back at Peter's house.   So many came to seek him out: there was no room in the house or even outside the front door.

Jesus was talking to those inside the house and answering their questions, when four people arrived carrying, on a mat, a person who was severely handicapped.

Because of the density and noise of the crowd, there was no way they could get Jesus' attention from outside, so they went up onto the flat roof of the house.   Knowing which room below Jesus was in, they lifted part of the roof and when they had made a large enough opening, they lowered the mat on which their physically handicapped friend was lying.

Recognising how much trust they were putting in his power to heal, Jesus spoke with compassion to the cripple:

> *My dear friend whatever it is that made you like this is forgiven!*

Some of the teachers who often spoke in the synagogue, heard Jesus say this and started talking quietly among themselves:

How can he say these things?

Is he trying to take the place of God?

Isn't God the only one who can overlook and decide to ignore wrong?

Jesus, aware of the question, said:

> *Why are you raising these sort of issues?   What should I have done—said to this physically handicapped person, **what has made you like this has been put right by God.**   Or should I have just said, **Get up! Roll up the mat!   Go away home!***

He said to the teachers:

> *I really do have the authority to tell people that what has kept them away from God has been put right and they are now free to live like the people God intended them to be when they were born!   But if it helps you, I will use your words.*

Jesus said to the paralytic:

Get up!

Roll up the mat!

Go away home!

The person got up, picked up the mat, and walked out in front of everyone. All were amazed and gave credit to God for what they were witnessing. *We have never ever seen anything quite like this before!* they said to one another.

Jesus went out and walked along the shore of the sea.   It wasn't long before a large crowd had gathered round him.   He talked to them and answered their questions.

Along the seaside path, Jesus saw Matthew sitting in a customs toll booth collecting taxes.   He said to him:

Come with me!

Matthew got up and joined Jesus and his friends.

Later Jesus and his companions were eating together.   A number of Matthew's friends were there too.   They were tax collectors working for Herod Antipas.   Nobody liked these people!

There were others there also who, like the tax collectors, were Jews in name only and had given up any attempt at living by the rules and regulations of Jewish belief.

The leaders of the synagogue saw Jesus eating with this group and asked his companions:

Why does Jesus, who is so religious, eat with these people who do not care at all about religion?

Jesus overheard their questions and answered:

You remember the proverb: **The healthy do not need to go to a doctor for help, only those who are sick?**

I did not come here to invite those to join me who are already living close to God.   I came to ask people like this to consider living with God in mind!

John's friends and some of the Pharisees often fasted to show they were serious about religion, and to help them be more focused about their faith. Some people who were talking with Jesus asked:

Why do John's followers and some of the Pharisees often fast but your friends never do?

Jesus replied:

> *At the time of a wedding, the bridegroom's friends do not need to keep any of the religious observances or the festivals. They can celebrate and enjoy themselves throughout this time. When it's all over and the bridegroom takes up his new life then they can fast!*

> *There is no use patching a well-worn shirt with a new piece of material. The new bit will shrink and tear a bigger hole when the garment is next washed.*

> *There is no point in storing new wine in wineskins which are old and hardened inside. The wine will continue to ferment, mature and stretch the skins. If there is no elasticity left, the skins will burst, the wine will be lost, and the skins ruined!*

> *New wine must always be stored in new wineskins!*

One Saturday, the sacred day, Jesus and his friends were walking through a wheatfield. As they walked, his companions picked some of the fresh grain to eat as a snack.

Some Pharisees seeing this asked:

Why are your friends doing this?

It's Saturday and no-one is allowed to prepare food to eat in this way.

Jesus replied:

> *Do you remember the story in the Hebrew Bible?* (I Samuel 21: 1–6)

> *David was on the run from those who wanted to kill him and came across a place of worship. He asked for food, but there was none except bread on the table in front of the shrine. It was the offering dedicated to God! David and his friends then ate the bread which was reserved for priests only.*

*We humans were not born to have our lives controlled by the rules and regulations which make Saturday a sacred day for us—**no!***

This day is sacred to help us remember God and to live better lives.

So Jesus, God's representative, was able to reinterpret religious practices like this and give them a new and better meaning.

When he returned to the synagogue, there was a person there whose hand had been so badly injured it could not be used.   The synagogue leaders kept a close eye on Jesus to see if he was going to heal on a sacred day: if he did, they were out to accuse him of wrongdoing.

Jesus said to the person:

Stand up!

Come out to the front where you can be seen!

He then asked the people:

What are we allowed to do on Saturday, this day set aside for the worship of God?

Do only what is good?

Do harm to others?

Restore life or destroy it?

There was silence!

Jesus looked around the gathering with a growing sense of anger mingled with deep sadness—no-one had compassion, all seemed insensitive and unable to respond.

He then said with anger in his voice:

Stretch out your arm and let's see your hand!

He did!

Immediately the hand was healed and restored to its original condition!

The leaders immediately left the synagogue and went straight away to find the representatives of Herod Antipas: they wanted to discuss the possibility of getting rid of Jesus.

Jesus and his friends walked down to the lake. A lot of people came after him. There were people from Galilee, Judea, Jerusalem, from south of Jerusalem, across the Jordan River and from the cities of Tyre and Sidon. They came because his popularity had spread so far.

As there was a danger the movement of the crowd would push him into the water, he asked his friends to launch a small boat.

He had healed so many people that all who were sick wanted to get close enough to be able to touch him.

Whenever people who were disturbed in any way came to Jesus for help, the evil spirits which possessed them would bring them to their knees and they would shout out: *Leave me alone, you son of God!*

Jesus always warned the spirits not to disclose his identity.

Jesus then decided to climb a mountain and asked his companions to go with him. While on the top, he formed them into a group to be his companions, to share his insights and thinking with others, to have the power to deal with all who were disturbed in any way and to heal those in need.

The members of this close group of friends selected by Jesus were:

Simon whom Jesus later nicknamed *Peter* (a word which means rock);
James and **John**, Zebedee's sons, nicknamed *Boanerges* or thunderbolts;
Andrew;
Philip;
Bartholomew;
Matthew;
Thomas;
James son of Alphaeus;
Thaddaeus;
Simon, nicknamed the *Eager One*;
Judas, nicknamed *Iscariot*, a word meaning fanatic (who later turned him over to the authorities).

Back at Capernaum, Jesus was again confronted by a large crowd. Their needs were pressing and they were so demanding of his time, he became busy and there was no opportunity to take a meal.

When his relatives heard about what he was doing, they came to get him— they thought he was out of his mind and sought the chance to bring him under control.

There was a lot of speculation about the nature of the power which seemed to drive him. Some of the experts from Jerusalem came to observe and concluded:

He is under the control of Beelzebub

and

He is forcing out evil spirits in the name of the head demon.

Jesus responded by calling the experts over to where he was sitting and challenged them, asking questions like:

How can Satan, the adversary, drive out Satan?

He also made comments like:

If ministers of the government who are in charge of running a country fall out with each other, the government will not be able to stay in power!

A family whose members cannot get along with each other, will soon break up!

If Satan fights Satan, that will be the end of Satan!

No-one can break into the home of an important person to rob them of their possessions without first overpowering everybody in the house and tying them up—only then can the house be looted.

Let me tell you bluntly, any of the things you say, no matter how offensive or deeply disturbing they are, can be overlooked and forgotten. But whoever ridicules God completely alienates themselves from God and that cannot be overlooked or forgotten!

Remember all these things were said because the experts concluded, ***his life was under the control of an evil spirit***.

Then his mother and his brothers arrived and stood waiting for him outside the house.   Eventually they sent a message to him, asking that he come out and talk with them.

There were quite a number around him inside as he was told, *Your mother, brothers and sisters are outside waiting to talk with you!*

Jesus replied, looking around at the circle of people seated in the room:

> *My mother and my brothers—who are they?*

> *All these people are family to me!*

> *Anyone who accepts the invitation to live with God in mind, is family to me—is brother, sister and mother!*

On the next occasion that Jesus was on the shore of the sea of Galilee, a large crowd gathered.   The number of people became so large he took to a boat and spoke to the people while sitting in the stern—everyone then had the chance to see and hear him!

Jesus spoke using a startling new method of attracting attention. What he said made people listen, but it also left a deep impression on them.   Here is an example of what he taught and said:

> *Pay attention to my words!*

> *A farmer planted seed across a field. Whilst he was scattering the seed in the usual way, some of the seeds fell on the path that ran alongside: the birds were quick to eat this seed.*

> *Some of the seeds landed on rocky outcrops where there was hardly any soil. After a few days, the seed started growing but the soil didn't hold moisture.   The hot sun soon dried up the plants.*

> *Some seed landed among thorn bushes—when they began to grow the thorns soon choked off the stalks of grain.*

> *The rest of the seed fell where it was supposed to, onto the soil which had been prepared.   When the plants grew, a part of the field produced thirty times as much as was scattered, a part sixty and a part, more than a hundred times.*

He finished with a comment which quickly became a punch line in his story-telling:

Anyone with two good ears had better hear what I say—it might make a difference to the way you live!

His companions—his inner circle of close friends—didn't understand why he was telling stories like this.

As soon as they were alone, thcy asked him how the stories were meant to be understood.   Jesus explained:

I will tell you in a straightforward way about the presence of God in our world and how we can experience this presence.

To others however, I will tell a story everyone can identify with and then leave it to them to draw their own conclusions as to what it says about God, and the presence of God in our world.

The reason why I tell stories in this way was given a long time ago by Isaiah who said:

The people may look wide-eyed but they may never see; they may listen intently, but never really understand what they hear; if they did, they would straight away turn their lives around and God would overlook what they had done and receive them back (6: 9 10).

To help his companions understand the stories he had told, Jesus gave an example based on the story of the farmer.

He began by saying that if they did not understand what that story meant, then they would never understand the others he was going to use.

This was his explanation:

The farmer is really scattering the message that God is a reality and can be experienced as a living presence in our world.

The seed stands for all who will hear this message.

The power of evil which pervades our world prevents some from really hearing the message. This is the seed which falls on the path which the birds eat.

The seed which falls on the rocky outcrops stands for all who hear the message and enthusiastically respond. When the going gets tough however, they soon give up on the message. It makes life too difficult for them.

The seeds which fall among the thorns stand for those who mix up the importance of the message about God's presence with the need to succeed in life and make money. They get so busy they haven't time to spend on dealing with the relevance of God's presence in their lives, so that they never get started on a religious life and their spirituality is neglected.

The seed which falls on the prepared soil stands for the people who do listen and understand!

Here is a story about light that Jesus once told:

There is surely no one around who would light up a lamp and then put it out of sight under a basket used for carrying seed or put it under a bed.

The right thing to do is to light up and then put the lamp on a stand so it will give light to the whole room. Everything hidden by the dark will then be exposed for everyone to see.

There is no secret which will remain a secret: everything will eventually come out into the open!

Anyone with two good ears had better hear what I say—it might make a difference to how they live!

There was another story involving seeds:

The presence of God can be experience like this:

A farmer sows the seed in a field, scattering it in the usual way. When he is finished, he goes off to bed. The next day he goes about his business in the normal way. This continues day in and day out and all the time the seed grows—it breaks the surface of the soil and eventually grows into a plant.

The farmer doesn't understand how growth takes place. It is the quality of soil which enables the seed to sprout, grow into a plant and eventually produce grain of its own. At harvest time, the farmer cuts with a sickle the stalks of grain!

This story about mustard seed was another Jesus told:

How can we discover where and how God is present in our world?

Listen to what I have to say. What happens when a mustard seed, the smallest seed in the whole world, is planted? Doesn't it grow larger than any other plant? Its branches are large enough for birds to nest among its leaves.

These are just some examples of the storytelling Jesus used when he was talking with people. He was an outstanding communicator and always used stories like this, then later would tell his companions what he meant.

One evening after a day spent talking with the people, Jesus decided to cross the sea of Galilee by boat.

Leaving the people behind, Jesus and his friends began to row across the water—there were some other boats also involved.

Out on the lake, a squall suddenly blew up. The wind was so wild, the water so rough, the boat got tossed about and started leaking. Jesus was sleeping on the stern seat.

His friends woke him up, shouting:

Teacher, aren't you concerned the boat will sink and we'll all be drowned?

Jesus woke and stood up. Looking around, he spoke sharply to the wind and shouted at the waves—*Be quiet!*

The wind dropped and it became very quiet.

Why did you panic? Jesus asked his companions: *Don't you go about aware God is with you?*

They all found the experience awesome and began to ask each other:

Who is this person—even the wind and the sea respond to his words!

Across the other side of the sea, they landed at Gerasenes.

As Jesus was climbing out of the boat a deeply disturbed person with a mental disorder, came rushing up to Jesus from a nearby cemetery.   He was completely uncontrollable.   When he was restrained by chains and leg irons, he broke them off.   Night and day he was in the cemetery or roaming the hills nearby, continuously shouting out and sometimes trying to take his life by cutting his body with stones.

When the man saw Jesus, he recognised him as a special person and rushed up to him.

Hearing the name **Jesus**, he started shouting,

Jesus, son of the living God (he meant a person who lived very close to God and was holy), *why are you here?   Why come after me in this way? In God's name, don't hurt me!*

He only said this because Jesus had ordered him to *shut up* and the evil spirits haunting him had responded.

What is your name? Jesus asked.

The spirits, not the man, answered: *We are **Many***.

There was more than one evil spirit living in this man's body.   That's why his behaviour was so violent!

The spirits then began to bargain with Jesus about their release.

A large herd of pigs was feeding on a nearby hillside.   The spirits asked:

If you want us to leave this man's body, let us enter into the bodies of those pigs!

Jesus agreed.

The spirits left the man and entered the pigs.

They stirred up the herd so much with their movement that two thousand rushed down the steep side of the hill, over the bluff, and fell straight into the waters of the sea where they drowned.

Those responsible for looking after the pigs quickly ran off into the nearby villages and farms round about to tell others about what had happened.

Those who heard the story came to see for themselves. They found Jesus and the man who had been so deeply disturbed, sitting quietly with him. He was fully clothed and calm. The people were overcome with awe and astonishment.

As news of the incident spread more people arrived to see the man and the pigs. When they realised the enormity of what had happened, they urged Jesus to leave their area as quickly as possible.

As Jesus got into the boat, the man asked if he could go with them. Jesus refused.

> *Go away home and find your family! Tell them what God has done for you and tell them about the kindness of God!*

The man did just that and visited the ten cities in his home area, telling whoever would listen about what Jesus had done. The story he told caused amazement!

Jesus crossed the sea of Galilee.

When he landed back on the other side, a large crowd gathered. The president of the Synagogue, whose name was Jairus, approached Jesus and fell on his knees imploring him:

My young daughter's dying! Please come and touch her so she can be made well. I don't want her to die!

Jesus agreed to see her so they left the shore, making their way towards the house of Jairus.

The crowd went along too and was soon making it difficult for him to get to the house.

A woman with a feminine disorder which had troubled her for twelve years, was amongst the people around him. Many visits to the doctor over the years had not brought either a cure or relief from pain. She had no money left and her health was getting worse by the day.

The woman knew all about Jesus and was at the front of the group behind him.

She gently touched the corner of his coat, thinking to herself:

If I touch this much of him, maybe I will be healed.

As soon as she touched his clothes she felt a change surge through her body.   She knew at once she was healed!

Jesus was aware that someone in need had touched him and turned around, demanding:

Who touched me?

His companions were beside him and responded:

Look at the number of people around us, all milling about and pressing close.   Why do you ask about someone touching you?

But Jesus turned around, looking carefully at everyone, seeking the person who had touched him.

The woman knew what had happened and became afraid.   She was trembling all over and fell on her knees in front of him.   She told him everything about herself.

Jesus said to her:

You are healed!   Your pain is gone!   You are well because you are aware God is with you.   God's peace go with you!

While the two of them were talking, word was brought to Jairus that his twelve-year-old daughter had died.

Don't worry Jesus about her, the messenger said, *Come home and prepare to bury her.*

Jesus overheard and said gently to Jairus:

Don't panic.   God is with you!

Jesus asked Peter, James and John to go with him to the house.

There were now so many people there and it was quite noisy as funeral preparations had begun.

Jesus went into the house and shouted:

> *Why have you begun mourning? The child has not died. She's asleep!*

His words were greeted with jeering and laughter.

Jesus sent everyone out of the house and took Jairus, the girl's mother and his three friends into the room.

Taking the girl by the hand he said in a strong voice:

> *Talitha, koumi!*—**little girl! get up!**

She did, and began walking around.

Her parents and Jesus' companions were overcome with astonishment.

Jesus told them not to talk to others about what had happened.

> *Give her something to eat!* Jesus told her parents.

Jesus left the area around the sea of Galilee and went to his hometown of Nazareth. His companions went with him.

The next Saturday (the sacred day), he went to the synagogue and was asked to comment on the reading from the Hebrew Bible.

People attending were very impressed and began asking:

Where does he get all this knowledge from?

Who gave him the authority to heal in the way he does?

Isn't he a craftsman—and Mary's son?

James, Joseph, Judas and Simon are his brothers. His sisters still live here in this town.

As the conversations continued, jealousy emerged.

Jesus, hearing what was being said and realising what was happening, commented:

> *All who speak on behalf of God are listened to, respected and honoured all over the place except on their own home ground and among family.*

It wasn't possible to help needy people, but Jesus did manage to heal some sick. He was astonished however at the lack of trust in God that the people showed.

For a time, however, he used Nazareth as a centre for touring towns and villages nearby.

Some time later, he brought his companions together. The twelve were sent away in pairs to visit in the neighbourhood and specifically to deal with people who considered themselves possessed.

He instructed them:

> *Take a walking stick with you, but don't worry at all about taking food, backpack or even purse.*
>
> *Wear sandals, but don't take changes of clothes.*
>
> *When you are received into a home, make it your base and work from there until you are finished in the area.*
>
> *If it is clear you are unwelcome and people don't want to listen to what you have to say, make obvious your displeasure at the edge of the town or village by publicly shaking the dust of that town or village from your sandals.*
>
> *This is a warning you are treating everybody there as non-Jews!*

They all left and followed his instructions. When they returned, they reported successful healings. They also told him they had healed the sick by rubbing olive oil on their bodies.

Jesus' popularity spread around the whole region. Everyone seemed to know about him, even Herod Antipas. Naturally there was a lot of speculation about his identity.

Some thought Jesus was John risen from the dead because that's how he could do all these astonishing things.

Others started a rumour saying Jesus was Elijah, the one who was believed to be the forerunner of God's representative, the Messiah.

He was also identified with other figures from the Hebrew Bible.

When Herod caught up with the gossip, he was conscience-stricken:

This has to be John, back to haunt me.   I had him executed but now he has come back to life!

The background for his troubled conscience is this:

Herod Antipas married Herodias, his brother Philip's wife, under very questionable circumstances.

John, the conscience of the nation, remonstrated with him: *It's totally improper for you to marry Herodias—look whose wife she really is.*

Herodias was most upset when she heard what John said.   To put her in good humour, Herod imprisoned John.

However, Herodias wasn't satisfied with imprisonment and wanted John eliminated.   But she could not fabricate a reason because Herod was scared of John and did not want to do him any harm.

So far as he was concerned, John had really done nothing wrong; moreover he was very religious and highly respected.   He didn't always agree with John or understand him but he often listened to what he had to say and thought very carefully about his words.

One day Herodias got her chance to dispose of John.   Herod celebrated his birthday and invited all the important people from the military and government administration.   Anyone of any social importance was there.

Herodias' daughter danced to entertain Herod and his guests, as was the custom.   She did so well, Herod was moved rather rashly to give her an open cheque:

Ask for anything, he said, *and it will be yours for the asking—I offer you up to half the kingdom, should you ask,* he added.

The girl sought advice from her mother.   *What do you think I should ask for?*

Herodias replied: *The head of John!*

The girl went back to Herod with the request: *I would like the head of John brought to me on a plate—now!*

Herod Antipas was really upset, but he could not break the promise he had made in front of all his important guests, without looking a fool.

So he reluctantly gave instructions for one of the prison warders to execute John.

The execution took place: the head of John was placed on a plate and handed over to the girl and she gave it to her mother.

This is why Herod Antipas had such a guilty conscience and mistook Jesus for John.

When John's friends heard what had happened, they collected his body from the prison and gave it a proper burial.

After Jesus' friends returned from their assignment, they talked to him about everything they had done and had taught.

There were so many people making demands on Jesus and realising they needed a break, he proposed they went off to a place where they could be alone and where they could talk over what had been happening in their lives.

They took a boat along the sea of Galilee, making for such a place.

Unfortunately, many of the people who still wanted to attract the attention of Jesus worked out where he and his friends must be going. They followed the path around the shore and were soon joined by others who also wanted to hear Jesus. The people moved so quickly on foot that they arrived at the place before the boat.

When Jesus got out, he saw the crowd. He knew from their reaction they were like people without a leader. He felt sorry for them and so settled down to talk to them.

Just before evening fell, his friends said to him:

This place is fairly isolated and it won't be long before it's dark. Why don't we encourage the people to leave now— perhaps on the way back to their homes they can buy something to eat from the farms or from the shops in the villages they pass.

Jesus had another plan:

You *could organise food for them!*

You must be joking! they replied with laughter.

It would cost at least six months' wages to buy enough bread to feed this lot!

How much food is available to start with? Go and find out! Jesus ordered:

Here is what we have found: was their reply—*five small round loaves and two fish!*

Ask the crowd to sit down on the green grass in groups, Jesus replied.

The people carried out the instructions and organised themselves into groups of a hundred and groups of fifty.

Jesus took the five loaves and the two fish, looked up into the sky and said the blessing.

He then broke the bread into pieces, and his friends took the pieces to the groups and distributed them amongst the people.

Jesus divided the two fish, and the pieces were distributed in the same way.

When all the people had finished eating, twelve baskets of leftover bread and fish were counted.

Five thousand people were involved in this meal.

Straight away, Jesus sent his companions off by boat to Bethsaida.

He stayed behind to farewell the people and then sought a quiet place on the side of a mountain to think things over—and to pray.

Later that night while he was still on his own the boat was out on the sea. His friends were rowing hard against a head wind but making very slow progress, trying to cross the water.

Just before dawn around 3.00 a.m., Jesus caught up with his friends. He was walking on the top of the water and about to pass the boat when his friends, seeing him, started screaming.

They thought he was a ghost and were very, very frightened!

Jesus called out:

Don't be afraid. It is me! Jesus! Don't be so upset!

He climbed into the boat and joined them. The wind fell and the water was calm.

Jesus' friends were dumbfounded and did not know what to think. They did not at all understand the incident of the loaves.

Jesus and his friends landed near Gennesaret. As soon as their feet touched the shore, word went out that Jesus had arrived. Quickly the sick were organised and brought to see Jesus wherever he went—village, town, farm or marketplace.

It did not matter where, the sick were brought to him for healing. *It's enough,* they said, *for the sick to just touch the edge of his coat and they will be healed.*

Everyone who touched his coat was immediately healed: that is true!

Some Pharisees and scholars from Jerusalem joined Jesus.

The first thing they noticed was that some of his friends did not wash their hands before starting their meals.

It is important to know that Pharisees and Jewish people in general would never dream of eating a meal without washing their hands and arms as far as the elbow.

Food bought from the marketplace must also be thoroughly washed.

They also wash cups, jugs, food bowls, sleeping mats and other things: all this is done in accordance with instructions given centuries ago and which can now be read in the Hebrew Bible.

With this background in mind, the rest of the story can be understood.

The Pharisees and their colleagues asked Jesus:

Why do your companions eat without washing their hands?

Why don't they live according to regulations set out for us by our ancestors?

Jesus replied:

You talk a lot of rubbish!

How can you be sincerely religious when all you want to do is talk about keeping rules and regulations!

Isaiah was thinking of people like you when he wrote:

> **All you ever do is talk about me.**
> **But you never think about me!**
> **It is stupid to worship me,**
> **and insist on following to the letter**
> **rules and regulations**
> **made up by other humans** (29:13).

If you take Isaiah seriously, aren't you putting the emphasis on human traditions and ignoring what God wants?

Didn't Moses say:

> **Respect your parents** (Exodus 20:12; Deuteronomy 5:16).

And again, didn't he write—

> **All who say bad things about their parents will surely die** (Exodus 21:17).

But don't you agree to family members giving huge donations to religious charities rather than support their own ageing parents.

They say they are giving it to God and you agree!

So don't your policies negate what God has said?

You put human tradition before God's words and then after a while you say the tradition is what God wants!

You are forever doing things like this and the people suffer.

When there was an opportunity, Jesus gathered a crowd around him and said:

Listen to what I say and try to understand.

*The food you eat doesn't make you in any way unfit to **live with** God. Nor does it make you unfit to **work for** God in the community—even if you haven't prepared the food in the correct way.*

It is what people say and talk about that makes them unfit to live with or work for God.

Later when Jesus and his companions were alone inside the house, they asked him what he actually meant by these words.

Jesus replied:

Haven't you worked out what I mean?

It's obvious enough isn't it?

The food you eat can't possibly make you unfit to work for God. Food goes into the stomach and eventually out of the body into a toilet: none of what you eat affects what you think!

By saying this, Jesus meant a person could eat what they like and eat it in any way they like, using whatever preparation they preferred at the time.

Jesus went on to say:

It's what a person thinks and then says and does which determines whether or not they are fit to work for God.

Out of the depths of the mind comes evil of every kind:

sexual promiscuity and immorality;

deceitful pilfering, murder;

unfaithfulness in personal relationships:

a lust for greed and power at the expense of others;

a deep desire to hurt and harm others, cunning deceit;

behaviour aimed at deliberately shocking and offending others;

attempts to destroy the success and happiness of others and give them the evil eye;

insults against others (slander) and insults against God;

an inner contempt for others which shows itself in pride and arrogance;

and hypocritically playing the fool religiously and morally.

These are the things which remove a person's right to work with God—and these are all things which come from deep inside a person.   This is what makes them unfit!

Jesus moved away to stay near Tyre.   He did this to get some peace.   He thought if he went somewhere he wasn't known, he would be left alone.

But people in the area soon discovered he was there.

One person who sought him out had a daughter who was mentally disturbed.

She knelt in front of him.   The woman was not a Jew, but a Greek from Phoenicia.

She pleaded with Jesus to do something to help her daughter.

Jesus refused and said, hoping to get rid of her:

I want to make sure the children are fed first.   I am not going to take food off their plates or out of their mouths to give it to dogs like you non-Jews.

But she had a very quick response:

Sir, she said, *the dogs under the table are allowed to eat the bits of food dropped onto the floor by the children at mealtimes!*

Jesus answered:

You are quite right!   I shouldn't have said what I did!

Go home—your daughter is healed!

When the woman arrived back at her home, she found her daughter was well and lying quietly on her bed.

Jesus left Tyre and set out for the sea of Galilee, travelling by way of Sidon.   He passed through the area known as the ten cities.

A person who was profoundly deaf was brought to Jesus.   Everyone urged him to touch the person because he could hardly talk.

Jesus took the person away from the crowd.   He put his fingers into the ears.   He put spit on his fingers and then touched the person's tongue.

Looking up to the sky, he gave a deep sigh and said:

Ephphatha—open!

At once the person was able to hear, and very soon was able to learn to talk quite clearly.

Jesus urged people not to make a fuss about what he had done.

It seems, however, that the more he asked people to say nothing, the more they talked about him.   They were overcome with astonishment and awe.

What he does, they said, *is done so well that a stone deaf person can hear and learn to talk!*

Wherever Jesus went crowds gathered around.

There was another occasion when everyone got carried away, forgot about the time and had problems when it came to food.

Jesus spoke with his companions about the difficulty which had arisen:

> *I am upset at the situation that's occurred,* he said.   *Many of these people have been with me for three days and appear to have run out of food.   Some have come quite a distance. If we finish up now when they are already hungry, they might not make it back home.*

> His friends said, *The problem is even worse.   This is a remote place.   There is nowhere we can get food around here!*

> *How much food is there among the people?* he asked.

Just seven small loaves of bread, was the answer.

So Jesus told everyone to sit down.   He took the seven small loaves in his hands, gave the usual blessing, broke the loaves up into small pieces and asked his companions to pass the pieces out amongst the people.

A few small fish were also produced.   Jesus said the blessing over them too, divided them up, and asked his friends to pass them around in the same way as they had passed around the bread.

There was a crowd of about four thousand people involved and they had plenty to eat.   What was left over was placed in seven large baskets.

As soon as the people moved away, Jesus and his companions took a boat across the sea to the area of Dalmanoutha.

Again the Pharisees caught up with Jesus and tried to provoke an argument. They were out to set a trap for him by asking for some sign Jesus was in fact working with God.

Jesus groaned with frustration:

> *Why do you always go on about a sign from God?*

> *Why don't you accept me at face value, as I am?*

> *You will never get what you ask—even if you did, you wouldn't recognise a sign as a sign!*

Jesus turned his back and walked out on them, got into a boat and crossed the sea of Galilee.

But Jesus and his friends had forgotten to bring enough bread with them. His companions had only one loaf in the boat.

> When Jesus heard about it, he sighed:

>> *Be warned!   The Pharisees are like yeast—so is Herod Antipas!*

> His friends were a bit stunned by this comment.

> *Did he say that because we don't have enough bread?*   One said to another, *What is he really getting at?*

Jesus could see the effect his words were having and spoke up:

Why are you talking about bread?

Don't tell me you don't understand?

Surely it's not that difficult! You're not deaf, are you, nor blind?

How many baskets of scraps did you collect after I fed the crowd of five thousand? Jesus asked.

Twelve they replied.

And after I fed the four thousand?

Seven they replied.

So surely you know what I am getting at by now? Jesus asked.

As they were entering Bethsaida, a group brought a blind person to him and urged him to help simply by touching.

Jesus took the person by the hand and walked away from the village. He rubbed his saliva onto the person's eyes then he placed his fingers on the eyeball. He asked if anything could be seen.

I see what must be people, was the reply, *but it's still fuzzy. They're like stick figures walking around.*

Jesus again put his fingers on the eyes. The person stared intently for a few seconds and then said:

I see everything very clearly.

Jesus warned him:

Don't go into the village but go straight home!

The Journey to Jerusalem

Jesus and his friends set out walking towards villages near to Caesarea-Philippi.

As they were walking along chatting to each other, he suddenly asked:

What are people saying about me behind my back?

Who do they think I am?

Some think you are John come back to life, he was told.

Sometimes you are likened to Elijah.

Sometimes you are confused with one of the prophets.

Well, the big question is, Jesus commented, *what do you have to say about me?*

You are God's representative, the anointed one, the Messiah! Peter replied.

Don't talk like that outside our group, Jesus warned them.

Jesus then steered the conversation around to what might happen if he continued doing the things he did and if he continued talking in the way he did.

He talked about things that sometimes happen to people like him in his position—being hurt, being rejected, perhaps even death, all instigated by the religious leaders.

He talked about being raised from the dead. He then told them how he felt about working with God.

Peter got Jesus on his own and asked him not to talk like that again.

But when Jesus caught sight of the others standing and staring at the two of them, he put Peter firmly in his place.

Satan! he said looking directly at Peter, *Don't get in my way. When you talk like that, you are not in tune with God at all! You are speaking without God in mind!*

To the crowd who had gathered with his companions, Jesus said:

If you want to be among my friends, forget about your own plans for yourself and your life. To follow me, you must choose the path of suffering.

If you are out to protect yourself at all costs, you will finish up with nothing but if you commit yourself to my way of life and are willing to share with others the good news that God is really present in our world, then you will discover what life is really all about!

Tell me, do you really gain anything if the whole world should belong to you but you finish up living without God?   There is no way back from being in that position!

Don't be ashamed about me, what I say and what I do.   Look at the quality of the people around us!

*If you are embarrassed and even ashamed of me in these circumstances, then the person referred to in the **Book of Daniel** (in the Hebrew Bible) who will come at the end of time to usher in God's reign, and gather together all those who have been loyal to God—that person will be ashamed of you!*

Let me tell you quite frankly: some of you here with me today will still be alive when the end comes.

Six days later, Jesus, Peter, James and John climbed up a high mountain to be alone.

In the presence of the others, Jesus was changed as a person.   The clothes he was wearing became a vivid white.   They saw Moses and Elijah talking with him.

When the moment had passed, Peter stammered:

Master, this is a terrific time for us.

Can we build three monuments here?   One for each of you —Moses, Elijah and you.

Peter was so terrified at what he had seen, he started talking wildly.

A cloud came over and cast its shadow down onto them.   From out of the cloud, a voice declared:

This is my son!

I am very close to him!

I love him dearly!

Pay careful attention to what he says!

Looking around, they saw no-one at all, only Jesus.

As they walked down the side of the mountain, Jesus told his companions to say nothing about the incident.

He talked to them again about what he thought was going to happen to him.   He mentioned the figure spoken about in the Hebrew Bible in the **Book of Daniel**, and of his being raised from the dead; but they didn't understand what Jesus meant.

The words **raised from the dead** were a mystery.

They asked him:

> *Don't the experts say Elijah will be amongst us before God's messenger arrives?*

> *Of course!* said Jesus.

> *Elijah does came first to prepare the ground for the arrival of God's messenger.   But isn't it the case that the people treat badly all whom God sends?*

> *Elijah has already come and look at the way he was treated!*

> *It has happened just as God's spokespersons of old said it would.*

When Jesus and his companions came down to the foot of the mountain, they saw a crowd gathered around their other friends.   There was an argument in progress between them and the scholars.

People were surprised to see Jesus and hurried to welcome him.   He asked about the reason for the debate.

A voice from within the crowd which had been growing, answered:

> *Master, I brought my son to see you.   He is possessed by an evil spirit and can't talk.   Whenever he is attacked, he gets thrown onto the ground, foams at the mouth and grinds his teeth together with the pain.   He then goes stiff all over.*

I asked your friends to deal with the demon that causes all this, but they couldn't.

Jesus spoke in frustration:

Don't you people ever recognise the way in which God works? How long will it be before you understand what I have been trying to tell you?

Why should I even bother trying!

Bring the boy over here!

As soon as the boy was brought to Jesus, the demon inside him exploded, throwing the boy into convulsions. He fell onto the ground and began rolling over and over, foaming at the mouth.

How long has he been like this? Jesus asked.

Since he was a child. There have been times when he tried to kill himself in the fire or in water. You can see what a problem he is to himself and to us. Please help us if you possibly can, the father replied.

*Why do you say **if you possibly can**? It is all a matter of perspective: of seeing everything with God in mind!*

The father cried out:

I do see things that way—tell me where I am going wrong!

Jesus saw the crowd was growing by the minute so he said to the demon in the boy's body:

I demand that you leave this boy at once! Don't ever come back!

The demon inside the boy screamed. The body went into convulsions and then lay still. All was quiet. The boy looked as if it had all been too much for him and had died. Those standing in front of the crowd certainly thought so.

Jesus took his hand and helped him stand up!

Later, when everyone had gone and Jesus and his friends were back at their home base, they asked why they hadn't been as successful as Jesus.

He replied,

It's only by carefully thinking things through with God in mind that this sort of situation can really be dealt with.

They moved around Galilee as a group, travelling a lot on their own and spending time together.   Jesus talked often about the influence his work was having on the authorities—he was sure he would be killed.   But he was also sure of the resurrection of the dead.

Jesus' friends had a lot of difficulty understanding this sort of talk but they never had the courage to ask him to explain more clearly what he meant.

They came back to the house they used in Capernaum.   Once inside, Jesus wanted to know what some of them had been discussing in a rather agitated way whilst together.

The argument had been about leadership—who was going to lead if he was killed—so they did not want to speak up about it at all.

Jesus sat down and they all gathered around:

If you want to lead, you must forget about what you want to do yourself and seek to help others meet their own needs, he said.

One of the children was in the room and Jesus put his arm around the child and said:

It's a bit like this:

When you take a lot of notice of a child like this one and accept them in the way I am doing, you are following my example.

Actually, whoever accepts me is accepting not so much me, but God—the one who sent me, he added as an aside.

John, one of his companions, said:

Master we saw another person forcing demons out of people

and they were using your name. He wasn't associated with us so we told him to stop.

Why did you do that? was Jesus' response. *No-one is going to undermine me and what I do by trying to heal in my name.*

Anyone who is not working against us is supporting us!

Anyone who gives you water to drink because you are identified with me, God's representative, will certainly receive a reward.

But this will not be the case for anyone who wrecks the innocence of a little child. It would be better for them to have a heavy stone fitted to their necks and be thrown into the sea and die!.

If it is your hand which gets you into trouble, cut it off!

It would be to your advantage to have only one hand for the rest of your life than to have two and end up at the end in a slow-burning rubbish pit.

If it is your foot which is the cause of your trouble, chop it off!

It would be far better for you to be lame for the rest of your life than to have two good feet and to end up in the rubbish tip.

If your eye gets you into trouble, pluck it out!

*It would be to your advantage to go into the presence of God with only one eye than to have two and end up in that slow-burning rubbish pit where **the worms never die and the fire burns on forever** (Isaiah 66: 24)!*

Everyone who is serious about working with God must discipline themselves.

Loyalty is like salt and fire in the temple sacrifice; it makes a person acceptable to God. Salt by itself is good and salty; but if it loses its flavour or its power to preserve, then it's no longer of use.

In your own lives, be salty—keep your integrity and your

loyalty and be at peace with one another.

Jesus moved away from this area down to Judea and crossed over the Jordan river.

Wherever he went, people gathered in large numbers to listen. He always responded to them and talked about God and the significance of living with God constantly in mind.

The Pharisees approached and as usual wanted to try and trap him by asking about his views on particularly difficult subjects.

Is it right for a husband to divorce his wife? they asked.

Jesus replied by asking if Moses had anything to say about the question.

Yes he does, they replied.

The husband has to end the contract of marriage in writing and then he can send away his wife.

Jesus then said:

> *Moses expressed the regulation in that way because you always failed to understand what God really wants of you.*
>
> *In **Genesis** we read this:*
>
> > **At the beginning God created both male and female.** (1: 27).
> >
> > **That's why a young man leaves his parents to live with a young woman. When they have intercourse, the two people become one person.** (1:27; 2:24).
>
> ***What has been joined together in this very special way, by God, should never be undone at all.***

When Jesus and his companions returned for the night, they asked him to explain what he meant.

Jesus told them:

A man who marries in the way laid down in the book of Genesis and then divorces his wife to enter into a relationship with someone else, is not faithful to his wife and the agreement they have had.

If a woman divorces her husband to enter into a relationship with someone else, she too is unfaithful to her husband and the agreement they have had.

They brought children to Jesus for him to offer a blessing over them.   He would do this by laying his hands on them.   However, his friends tried to prevent this from happening.

When Jesus became aware of what was going on, he was angry:

Let the children continue to come to me!

Do not stop them!

It is children like these who help us understand God is really present in our midst.

I know that unless we are open, trusting and find it possible to forgive, we will not experience the reality of God's presence in our lives and in our world.

Jesus put his arms around the children and offered a blessing for each by placing his hands on their heads.

There is another story about Jesus.

Jesus was walking along a path and was confronted by a person who knelt in front of him.

Good Master, he asked, *what must I do to receive eternal life?*

Jesus bridled:

*Why do you try to flatter me by calling me **good** Master?*

Stop and think about what you are saying!

If you want a model to copy, then it is God: for only God is good!

Do you know the commandments?

Do not murder;

honour the personal relationships you enter into;

do not steal;

do not tell lies;

do not cheat;

give respect to your parents (Exodus 20: 12–16;
Deuteronomy 5: 16–20).

Master, was the reply, *I have lived my life by these principles since I was quite young.*

Jesus looked sharply at the man when he heard these words and warmed to him.

Then there is just one more thing for you to consider doing:

Go home and sell up everything and give the money you raise to the poor.

If you do this, God will richly reward you.

Then come, and be one of my companions!

When the man heard this advice, his face fell and he began to look extremely unhappy for he had a lot of money.

Slowly he walked away!

Jesus, who had been watching the reaction remarked to his close friends:

It is very difficult for all who have a lot of money to take God seriously.

They were astonished to hear him say this. Prosperity was a sign of God's blessing and a sign a person had worked hard.

Jesus, aware of the impact of his words, repeated them:

It will be very hard for the wealthy to join God's community. In actual fact, it will be far easier for a camel to get through the small door which is used when the main gate into the courtyard is closed (the needle door) than for a wealthy person to join God's community!

His friends were even more astonished.

The question which now arose and troubled them was:

If that's the case, how will anyone be able to join God's community?

Jesus looked intently at the group and said:

This may be impossible if you are thinking about what we have to offer God which is acceptable, but from God's point of view there are no barriers.

Peter jumped in:

Jesus, we have given up everything to join you and become your companions.

Jesus replied:

That's right!

Whoever gives up family, parents, their own children and even land, for me and the opportunity to help spread the news that God is really present among us, will receive their reward!

You will receive a hundred times as many houses, brothers, sisters, mothers, children and land than you have now—though you will be persecuted and suffer.

Many who are first now to hear all this may well come in last, and many who are among the last to hear, may be amongst the first to really respond.

The path went down towards Jerusalem and Jesus was out in front. But his companions who were coming along behind him were confused about what he had said: many of his other friends were frightened by his words.

Jesus took his companions aside and told them what was going to happen to him:

> *Listen carefully,* he said, *we are now quite near Jerusalem and to the time when I will find myself in the grips of the chief priests and the scholars.*
>
> *They will find a reason to sentence me to death and the Romans will carry out that sentence.*
>
> *They will spit on me in contempt, whip me and then kill me.*
>
> *But three days after I die, I will rise to life.*

Remember that figure in the **Book of Daniel**—Jesus was talking in that way because he was that figure!

It was then that James and John, Zebedee's sons, asked him—speaking to him on their own:

Master, we have a favour to ask from you.

Jesus replied:

> *Tell me what it is.*

They said:

When you are in a position of influence, we want to help you, so could one of us sit on your right side and the other on your left?

Jesus said slowly and thoughtfully:

> *Do you not have any idea what your question actually means?*
>
> *Are you prepared to be treated as badly as I will be, by drinking out of the same cup as I use?*
>
> *Are you prepared to suffer pain and hurt—to be immersed— in the same way as I will be?*

Yes! they enthusiastically replied.

Jesus responded:

> *Then you **will** drink from the same cup as I will and you **will** be immersed in the same way as me.   But I do not make*

decisions about who sits on my right or on my left: only God makes such decisions.

When the others heard of this conversation they were angry with James and John, and an argument broke out.

Jesus intervened and, calling them together into a group, said:

You know how secular rulers govern?   How they order their people around!   You know that the rulers' appointees have absolute power over the people and can do what they like!

Don't throw your weight around and act arrogantly like they do!

If you want to be a leader, you must work for the people.   Listen to them, try to help them and respond to their needs.

*If you want to be at the top, you must work with other people's interests in mind.   You do this, not by being out in front ordering everyone else around, but by being **with** the people.*

*I have **never** behaved like a slave master with you.   I have been the exact opposite.   I have behaved like a slave to each of you— even to the point of giving up my life to buy your freedom!*

Jesus and his friends visited Jericho.

When they came to leave, a large crowd went with them.   As they were walking along the path, they passed a blind beggar, Bartimaeus, the son of Timaeus, who was sitting nearby.

When he heard it was Jesus of Nazareth passing by, he began shouting as loudly as he could:–

Jesus!

Son of David!

Messiah!

Help me!

Those around him told him to *be quiet* but this only made him shout more loudly.

Jesus stopped.

> *Tell him to come over here to me!*

People then began to encourage Bartimaeus!

Get up!

He's asking for you!

Don't be scared!

Bartimaeus threw off his coat as he sprang to his feet and ran towards Jesus.

> *What do you want me to do for you?* Jesus asked.

Bartimaeus responded with excitement in his voice:

I want to see again!

Jesus replied,

> *Go on then—be on your way!*
>
> *You can see!*
>
> *You believe I can heal you—so you are well!*

At that moment Bartimaeus was able to see!

He then joined the crowd of people who were following Jesus.

Jesus in Jerusalem

Jesus and his companions were making their way towards Jerusalem. Near Bethany at Bethphage on the Mount of Olives, Jesus asked two of them to go on ahead. His instructions were:

> *At the next village just inside the entrance, you will find tied up to a post a young donkey that's not been broken in for riding. Untie it and bring it back to me. If anyone asks you why you are taking the donkey, reply,* **Its master needs it and will send it back here as soon as possible.**

The two went off and found the donkey tied up at the door of a house facing the street. As they were untying it some of the people who were there said:

What do you think you are going to do with the donkey?

They replied in the way Jesus had said, and no-one made further comment.

They took the donkey back to Jesus. Some coats were thrown over its back for a saddle and Jesus climbed on.

A procession formed and excitement began to mount. Some people spread their coats on the ground for the donkey to walk over. Others cut branches from nearby trees and formed an arch for him to pass under.

There were people in front and behind him and they were all shouting:

> ***Three cheers for Jesus!***
>
> ***Blessings on God's representative!*** (Psalm 118: 25–6).
>
> ***God bless King David's people!***
>
> ***Three cheers for God!***

Jesus entered through the gate of the city and went into the temple and looked at everything that was happening there.

As it was late in the afternoon, he went back to Bethany to spend the evening with his companions.

Next morning as Jesus and his friends left Bethany, he felt hungry. At a distance he saw a fig tree with leaves on it. He went to it as if expecting to find fruit. Naturally there was no fruit because Jesus went looking out of season for the figs.

Jesus was heard to say:

> *No-one will ever again eat fruit picked from this tree!*

They then walked on to Jerusalem and entered the temple.

It was then he began chasing the retailers and their customers from the area. He turned over the counters used by money changers and the tables used by the merchants who sold the doves used in sacrifices.

Then he held up all who were carrying containers of any kind through the area.   He kept saying to everyone:

Doesn't the Hebrew Bible say:

>**My house is a place to visit!**
>**My house is a place in which to pray!**
>**All the world will gather here!** (Isaiah 56:7).
>**You people have turned it**
>**into a hideout for thugs and thieves!** (Jeremiah 7:11).

The chief priest and the scholars heard what he said and began looking for a way to get rid of him.   But they were afraid of him.   It seemed to them everybody else was completely astonished at what he said and very impressed with him as a person.

As darkness fell, Jesus and his companions left Jerusalem to again spend the night at Bethany.

When Jesus' friends passed the fig tree the next morning, they saw it was dried up and looked dead from the roots up.

Peter recalled the words of Jesus the previous day and said:

Master, look at the tree you cursed—it's all dried up!

Jesus responded:

Learn to live the whole of your lives with God in mind!

*If you do and you never waiver, then you will be able to say to this mountain **move from here into the sea**: and it will!*

Everything you decide to ask God for, will come your way.

Just learn to see everything with God in mind as you think things through!

Whenever you stand to address your thoughts to God, you must overlook and put out of your minds all that others have done to hurt you, then God the Creator who's caring and compassionate will overlook and forget all your wrongdoing!

They continued to Jerusalem.

As they passed through the temple area, the chief priests, scholars and community leaders confronted him:

What right do you have to do the things you do?

Who gave you permission?

Who gave you the authority?

Jesus angrily retaliated.

I've got a question for you.   If you answer it, I will answer your questions!

Who gave John the right to offer ritual cleansing.   Did God give him this right or did he get permission from some other person?

They discussed it among themselves,

If we say God gave John the right, Jesus will ask us why we didn't accept what John did and said.

Many people on the other hand think John is one of God's spokespersons—so we can't say he got permission from some other person!

There were becoming anxious about the crowd which had gathered around, so they thought it wise to answer:

We don't know the answer to your question!

Jesus then responded:

Nor will I answer your questions!

Here is another good example of the stories Jesus told:

A farmer planted out a vineyard, hedged it in, dug a wine press, built a lookout, leased it out and then went overseas.

When the harvest was in, he sent one of his staff, a messenger, to collect his share of the income.

Those who had leased the land grabbed the messenger, beat him up and sent him away.

The owner sent another messenger.   This one was killed.

He kept on sending messengers.   Some went back injured; others never came back—they were killed.

The owner decided to send his own son, the apple of his eye, thinking:

When they see who it is I have sent, they will take notice and I will receive my share of the money.

But they said to each other:

This is the owner's son and some day he will inherit this vineyard, so let's kill him and take the land for ourselves!

So they grabbed the son, killed him and disposed of his body outside the vineyard.

What do you think the owner is going to do? Jesus asked them:

Yes, you are right!

He will now arrive and kill those who had leased the land and will rent the vineyard out to somebody else.

Do you remember what the Hebrew Bible says:

>**The stone rejected by the builders**
>
>**has become the most important stone of all.**
>
>**Look what God has done—it is so amazing!** (Psalm 118: 22–23).

The leaders knew Jesus was telling the story against them and they were angry.   They really wanted to arrest him, but they realised the crowd was on Jesus' side and they were afraid.   So they left him in the temple and withdrew.

The Pharisees met with some of Herod's advisers and discussed a trap they might set for Jesus, then they sent representatives to talk to Jesus.

When they found him, they said:

Master you are fair and honest!

You respect people and do not care a lot for your own status.

You talk much about what you believe God asks of us, so we have a question for you.

Should we who are Jews pay taxes to the Roman emperor or should we not?

Jesus was equal to the challenge.   He knew what the question was aimed at doing and commented:

Why are you trying to catch me out?

He then asked one of them to show him a coin.

When one was produced, he asked:

Whose picture is on the coin and what's the name underneath?

The emperor's, was the reply.

So what's the problem? said Jesus. *Pay the emperor whatever is owing to him and pay God whatever belongs to God!*

Those who had asked the question expecting to catch him out were amazed at the answer.

The Sadducees who were priests and worked with the Romans, did not believe people would rise from the dead.   Some of them came to Jesus with a question:

*Master, Moses wrote this in **Deuteronomy** (25: 5–10):*

> **If a married man dies without children, his brother must marry his widow and produce a family.   The eldest of the sons born will inherit the property and become the heir.**

Once upon a time, there were seven brothers.   The first died without having children.

The second married the widow but also died without a family.

The same thing happened to the third and so on until all seven had married the woman: then the woman died.

At the resurrection of everyone at the end of time, whose wife will she be—remember there were seven husbands involved.

Jesus replied:

Haven't you missed the point altogether?

You are really ignorant about the way passages in the Bible should be interpreted.

You don't really understand the power of God and the way God works!

When men and women are raised to life, it is no longer a question of who's married to whom.   All who are raised, take on a God-like form of body.

Moreover, don't you remember the story about Moses and the burning bush?

God spoke to Moses and said,

> **I am the God of Abraham, the God of Isaac and the God of Jacob** (Exodus 3: 6).

We are not talking about the God of the dead—we are talking about the God of the living!

You've got the interpretation all wrong!

A scholar approached while the Sadducees and Jesus were in deep discussion.   When he heard how Jesus handled such a difficult question, he had his own query:

Of all the rules and regulations given by Moses, which is the most important of all?

The most important, replied Jesus, *is this found in* **Deuteronomy**:

> **Pay close attention people of Israel.   God is God. There is no other God at all so you must be wholly**

committed in every possible way to working with God
(6: 4–5).

It's followed closely in importance by this statement, found in **Leviticus**:

Treat those who have any claim at all on you in the same way as you would wish them to treat you (19: 18).

Apart from these two references, there is nothing of similar significance and importance to be found in the Hebrew Bible.

The man said:

Master, I agree with what you say about God.

It's true we must live wholly committed to God.

We need to hold others in high regard and to accept and respect them in the same way as they accept and respect us.

I also agree that living with this basic principle in mind is far more important than any number of sacrifices and offerings we might make in the temple.

When Jesus heard these words, he realised what he was saying and commented:

You are really quite close to experiencing God's presence!

You are just about a member of God's community!

The crowd became quiet.   There were no more questions as the relevance of this conversation dawned on everybody!

Later, Jesus was in the temple porch teaching.   In the course of what he said he asked:

Why do scholars believe the Messiah will be a son—a descendant— of King David when God prompted David himself to say:

God said to the king:

> **sit here on my right**
> **and I make all your enemies**
> **into your slaves.**   (Psalm 110: 1).

Now I interpret this as a reference to the Messiah.   If this is so, how can the Messiah be both the king and the king's son?

The people listening were very impressed with the quality of what he said.

At another point, Jesus remarked:

Be wary of scholars.   They enjoy parading their learning by wearing long and colourful robes.

They like the attention people give them.

They claim front seats when they appear on public occasions.

They like to be seen at all important receptions and functions.

But they know how to rob the poor and exploit the defenceless.

They make a big show out of using long-winded prayers and in giving impressive speeches.

They are snobs!   They are revolting!

Because much is expected from them, they will be severely punished.   They fail to live up to the people's expectations!

Later still Jesus was relaxing sitting near the box where people placed their donations to help run the temple.

He noticed the wealthy were contributing well and then he watched as a very poor widow came up, searched in her purse for a contribution and then dropped a couple of coins into the box.

Her gift was worth only a few cents.

Jesus called his companions together and said to them:

This poor widow's contribution is of far greater value than all the money put into the box by those who were very well off.

All of these people put in money they didn't need.   This woman

*gave the last few cents she had in her purse.   Now she doesn't
have any money left to live on.*

As they were preparing to leave the temple, one of his friends said:

Master!   Look at these magnificent stones in these beautiful buildings!

He responded:

*Yes I see the stones and the buildings in this marvellous complex, but
I am certain they will not last forever.*

There will come a time when they will be destroyed, stone by stone!

They moved out onto the Mount of Olives and sat looking at the temple on
the opposite hillside.

Peter, James, John and Andrew managed to get him on his own.

*When will this destruction take place? they anxiously asked.   Can
you tell us what to watch out for, so we can be prepared?*

Jesus replied:

*Listen, it's important that no-one makes a fool out of any of
us!*

*Many people in the future will claim to be me.   My name
will be used and listeners will be deceived.*

*When you hear rumours about the beginning of a war or
are around when one breaks out, take courage.*

*Wars must happen and they will occur before everything
else happens.*

*There will be earthquakes all over the place, and severe
famines.   All this is just the beginning!*

Take your guard!

You will be hauled into the courts; you will be beaten up while attending synagogues; you will find yourselves having to give account of your lives in front of the authorities.

But rest assured, the end will not occur until the good news that **God is really here in our midst**, *is shared with everyone throughout the world.*

When you are arrested and taken to court, don't spend a lot of time and energy working out what you are going to say in your defence. The appropriate words will come at just the right moment!

Actually it won't be your own words you speak. What you say will come from the God who is present in your life.

Family members will fall out with each other, even to the point of betraying each other to the authorities and to certain death. Parents will turn on their own children and have them killed!

The truth is you are going to be hated, all because of me, because of what I have said and what I have done, and because of who I am.

But if you can hold on to your faith right to the end, God will be there to receive you and you will be blessed.

There's a lot more to say!

When you see that disgraceful statue standing in the temple where it shouldn't (the reader will be able to work out what this means), *then all who live around here should escape as quickly as possible to a remote hillside.*

No-one on the roof of their home should dash inside to gather their belongings.

If you happen to be out working in the fields, don't pause to retrieve the clothes you have taken off.

Pregnant women or women with babies and young children,

will have a bad time.

Just hope that all this upheaval doesn't take place in winter.

It will be the worst upheaval the world has ever experienced and nothing quite like it will ever happen again.

Actually, if God doesn't intervene to shorten this time of disaster and destruction, no-one will survive at all.

God will only intervene because God loves and cares about the people of choice!

*So if somebody shouts out, **Here is God's representative**, or, **There is God's representative**, don't take any notice!*

It's inevitable that people will come and go pretending to be God's representatives or genuine spokespersons for God. They may even fool people with the marvellous things they do, so even those in touch with God may be deceived.

But take up your guard!   Be really vigilant!

I have told you these things before they happen, to warn you!

> *At the time all of this happens,*
> *the sun will lose its heat and brightness,*
> *the moon will no longer be visible,*
> *planets will fall out of orbit,*
> *the stars will disappear,*
> *and the forces of nature*
> *will be thrown out of kilter.*
> *At that moment you will see the figure*
> *spoken about by Daniel*
> *emerge out of the clouds*
> *and enter the world,*
> *visible and impressive.*
> *Messengers will immediately be despatched*

*to gather the people God has chosen
from around the world!*

Let me give you an illustration of what I mean.

*When a fig tree bursts into bloom, you know it is nearly
summer!*

*So when you see all these things I have been speaking about
begin to happen you will know the time for God to personally
intervene is quite near.*

*Some of you listening to me will be around when all this
disintegration takes place.*

*The cosmos, universe and even the earth will be destroyed—
but my words will not be destroyed!*

Note well!

No-one at all knows when all this disintegration will begin.

*No-one in God's immediate presence nor in our world has
any inkling of when it will all begin.*

Take care!

Be watchful!

Always be at the ready!

This moment will sneak up without warning!

Take this story to heart:

*A person goes away and leaves their employees to look after
the house.*

*Each has a designated task and is instructed to be extra
careful. All await the return of the owner which may occur
at any moment;*

The owner may come in the evening, at midnight, just before dawn or sometime during the day, in the morning for example.

The point is, it will go badly for anyone who is asleep when the owner returns.

What the owner has said to the staff, I also tell you.

Be prepared at any moment for the end to come!

It was just two days before the Passover festival and the associated celebrations were about to begin.

The scholars were deep in consultation trying to set up a trap to arrest Jesus and if possible have him eliminated.

They were concerned how it could happen without causing a major upheaval.

We must do it before the festival otherwise things may get out of hand, they said.

Jesus had meantime withdrawn again to Bethany where he was staying with Simon who had at one time suffered from a terrible skin disease.

They were eating together when a woman came into the room carrying a pottery jar containing expensive, sweet-smelling perfume. Before anyone could react, she broke the jar and poured the perfume on the hair of Jesus' head.

There was an angry reaction from the people eating with Jesus:

This is an utter waste, they muttered. *The perfume could have been sold off at a handsome price and the money given to the poor!*

They abused the woman with the nasty things they said.

Jesus called for quiet, saying:

Leave her alone!

Why abuse her like this?

Hasn't she done something quite special for me?

The poor will always be around and you can contribute to their wellbeing at any time. But I will not always be with you.

This woman has, by what she has done, confirmed I will soon die!

I'll tell you something that will make your ears tingle:

*Whenever people talk about **God being really present among us,** this story will be recalled and told over and over again!*

At this point Judas, nicknamed the fanatic, one of Jesus' companions, went off to talk with the chief priests.

In the course of the discussion, he offered help to arrest Jesus. They were pleased to get this degree of assistance, especially from one of Jesus' close friends. They promised to pay him.

From that moment, Judas kept looking out for the right moment to keep his part of the bargain.

It was the first day of the celebrations and the lambs for the passover were being slaughtered in the temple.

His companions asked:

Jesus, where do you want us to go to prepare the passover meal?

He replied:

This is what you are to do.

Two of you can go into Jerusalem.

Enter at the gate we normally use and you will be met by a man carrying a water jar on his head.

*Follow him back to his house and ask the owner, **Our master wants to know if there is a room available where he and his companions can eat the Passover meal.***

The owner will then take you upstairs and show you a large furnished room which is ready to be used.

You can prepare the meal there.

The two friends went to Jerusalem and everything happened just as Jesus said it would.   They set to and prepared the meal.

Later in the evening while Jesus and his companions were sharing the meal, Jesus said,

One of you is going to make it possible for them to arrest me!

His friends were aghast that anyone should even think of doing such a thing.   Each in turn asked Jesus:

You are not meaning me are you?

> *Actually it is one of you who is dipping his bread into this bowl with me,* he replied.

He added.   *I will die, just as the Hebrew Bible says, but it is going to be terrible for the person who lets me down.*

> *It would have been better for that person if he had never been conceived!*

It was while they were still eating the meal that Jesus took in his hands some of the bread from off the table.   He blessed it with familiar words and broke it into pieces saying to his companions:

> *Take a piece of this bread!*

> *Eat it!*

> *It stands for me, for what I've done and for all the things we've done together!*

Jesus took a cup of wine from off the table, blessed it in the usual way and gave it to his companions to drink, saying

> *Drink from this cup!*

Each of them drank some of it.

Jesus then said:

The wine in this cup which you have drunk stands for my death.

My death symbolised by my blood is a sign of the relationship we have with God.

I will not drink again with you until I have drunk new wine in God's community.

They sang a psalm and then walked out onto the slopes of the Mount of Olives.

Jesus said:

You are all going to let me down.   It is just like the Hebrew Bible says:–

The shepherd will be struck down

and the sheep will scatter!   (Zechariah 13: 7).

But after I am raised from the dead I will go to Galilee where you can meet up with me.

Peter was indignant.

If all the others let you down, I will be the exception!

Jesus spoke again:

Before tonight is over, you will have told others you do not know me three separate times.

Peter was adamant:

To the point of death, I will never do that!

The others echoed Peter's words.

Jesus and his companions made for the garden known as Gethsemane.

When they arrived at the place where they usually went, Jesus said to the group:

Stay here.   I want to spend some time alone thinking about everything and talking with God.

Peter, James and John were asked to accompany Jesus to where it was quieter.

He was very sad and quite upset in himself.   He said to his close friends:

I am so upset I feel I want to drop dead!

Stay with me!

Keep me company!

Please don't go to sleep!

Jesus moved away a short distance and kneeling down they heard him say:

Creator God, compassionate and caring,
if it's at all possible don't let all this happen to me!
don't force me to go through with it by having me suffer in this way—
but do what you must!
I am committed to working with you!

When Jesus took a break, he sought encouragement from his companions nearby, but they were asleep.

He woke Simon whom he had nicknamed Peter, pleading:

Wake up!

Can't you last out for another hour?

You could spend the time praying!

When he received no response, he cajoled him:

What's about to happen will test your loyalty to me!

It'll be your life's ultimate test—you should prepare for it!

When there was no response again, Jesus said sadly:

Your heart is in the right direction but you are really not up to it, are you?

Jesus returned to the place he had chosen and prayed the same words as before.

When he returned, his friends had all fallen asleep, again.   They were so tired they couldn't keep their eyes open!   When they realised what had happened, they were speechless.

A third time Jesus prayed and returned to find them asleep.

You may as well sleep, he exclaimed, *and get rid of your exhaustion!*

But it was not to be.   There was noise of people moving about in the garden.

Jesus shouted:

It's all over!

I'm going to be handed over to the Romans!

Get up!

Let's get ready!

Look, here he comes!   That one who's going to let me down!

The words were hardly out of his mouth when Judas, who was going to let him down, arrived on the scene.   As one of Jesus' close friends, he knew where he would be and had arrived with a group armed with swords and clubs sent with him by the chief priests, the leaders of the community and the scholars.

Judas had briefed them just before they set out:

You should arrest the person whom I greet as a friend.   Secure him and take him away, he had told them.

So in keeping with the plan, Judas walked straight up to Jesus and affectionately greeted him, saying:

Master!

Jesus was immediately grabbed and arrested.

In the confusion, someone drew a sword and struck out at one of the high priest's own representatives.   His ear was cut off!

Jesus was heard to say:

> *Why have you come after me like this—with swords and clubs?*
>
> *Why treat me as if I am a criminal?*
>
> *I have been in the temple every day but you didn't arrest me when I was teaching out in the open?*
>
> *What's said in the Hebrew Bible, about me, must now happen!*

Jesus' companions all ran away into the dark.

One of his friends who was there only had a robe wrapped around his body.   As he was grabbed, he ran away naked leaving his robe behind in the hands of his would-be assailants.

Jesus was taken off to meet the high priest.   The chief priests, along with the community leaders and the scholars, got together and held a consultation.

Peter, keeping a safe distance, also arrived in the courtyard of the high priest's palace and sat down with the guards who were sitting around the fire keeping warm.

The chief priests and the Council which led the nation, set about trying to find witnesses to say something sufficiently damning against Jesus so they could recommend his death to the Roman Governor.

They were initially not able to find something on which all could agree. Too many lies were being told!

Finally the agreement came.   Some witnesses were prepared to testify with these words—

We overheard him say he could tear down the temple which we have built and in three days build another with his own hands.

But even then, no one person could agree with another on the detail.

The high priest who was presiding over the meeting stood and asked Jesus:

Is there anything you would like to say in your own defence?

You hear what these people are saying against you—why not speak up!

Jesus was silent!

After a while, the high priest asked—

Are you God's representative? The anointed one?   Blessed be God!

Jesus' answer was clear:

> *Yes I am!*

And then he added:–

> *Soon you will see me*
> *sitting at the right side of God*
> *in a position of power and influence.*
> *And later still you will see me*
> *coming again out of the clouds!* (Daniel 7: 13; Psalm 110: 1).

The high priest erupted angrily, tore his clothes as a sign of his anger and shouted:

We don't need to hear any more witnesses!

You hear him claim to be God!

Recommend what we must do!

They shouted back:

He is guilty of death!

Some of those present began to spit at him, expressing their complete disapproval of what he had said.

Then the guards blindfolded him and physically assaulted him.

Tell us, which one of us hit you? they asked.

Then they began to torture him with their violence.

Outside in the palace courtyard, Peter was still warming himself from the fire.

One of the high priest's servants—a young woman—came by.

She stared at Peter, and then said:

You're one of Jesus of Nazareth's friends, aren't you?

Peter was adamant.

No I'm not!

I don't know who you are talking about.

What an insulting thing to say!

He walked out to the gate and as he did, he realised he had let Jesus down.

He went back inside.

The girl again saw him.

He is one of them—I'm sure of it, she said to the others.

No I'm not! I have no connection with him! was the angry response.

Some time later the people with whom he was talking said:

You talk like a Galilean: surely you're one of them!

Peter was furious and lost his temper.   He shouted:

I don't even know the person you are talking about!

It was then he recalled Jesus saying to him some hours earlier:

> *Before this night is through, you will let me down.   Three times you will say you don't know me!*

Peter started to sob!

Early next morning there was a meeting involving members of the council which looked after the affairs of Judaism. Together the scholars, community leaders and the chief priests met.   They secured Jesus and sent him to

Pilate.

He asked Jesus:

Are you king of the Jewish people?

Those are your words! was the reply.

It was then the chief priest spoke against Jesus and explained the charges they wished to bring against him.

Pilate again questioned Jesus:

Do you have anything to say for yourself?

Don't you take seriously what these people are saying against you?

Jesus was silent!

Pilate was astonished at the reaction he was receiving.

At this particular festival, Pilate always released a prisoner who was given their freedom at the request of the people of Jerusalem.

In prison at that time was Barabbas who had been arrested with some others for murder, after a riot had been put down.

The people now came to Pilate with the request he free a person according to established custom.

Pilate seized the opportunity to try and save Jesus for he realised the chief priests were jealous of his popularity.

Do you want me to free the king of the Jews? he asked.

The chief priests had anticipated this possibility and had said to the people:

If he gives a choice, choose Barabbas.

So they began to shout back:

Barabbas!   Barabbas!   Barabbas!

Pilate again pleaded with them:

Do you want me to free the man you call king of the Jews?

The crowd screamed:

Crucify!

Crucify!

Crucify!

Pilate shouted back.

Why?—Why?   What wrong has he done?

The crowd chanted even louder:

Crucify him!

Crucify him!

Pilate had no option.   He wanted to keep on-side with the people, so he made his decision:

Barabbas to go free!

Jesus to die!

He ordered his soldiers to prepare him for public execution with a severe flogging.

The soldiers responsible for such executions took Jesus inside the Antonio Fortress where they got a group of their friends together.

In the courtyard they humiliated him to destroy his confidence and to undermine his courage.

He was dressed in a purple soldier's robe and a crown made out of branches from a thorn bush was thrust on his head, making him look like a king.

They taunted him laughing and shouting:

*So, **you** are the king of the Jews?*

Some king you look!

They struck him around the head with a stick, spat at him and mocked him, kneeling in front of him pretending to show their allegiance.

When they grew tired of making fun of him and humiliating him, and thought his confidence had been sufficiently undermined, they took back the purple robe, gave him his own clothes to wear.

They then removed him to the place where crucifixions were held.

Simon from Cyrene in Africa was just entering the city, having earlier left his farm and home to join the festival in Jerusalem.

The soldiers saw him and forced him to carry the crossbar to be used in the execution.

Simon was the father of Alexander and Rufus.

The place where the soldiers took Jesus for execution is called Golgotha, the place of the skull.

They offered him wine mixed with a drug to give him relief from the pain to follow: but he refused to drink it.

They nailed Jesus to a cross!

The soldiers then tossed dice to see which one of them would take his clothes.

It was 9.00 a.m. when Jesus was nailed to the cross.

A notice was fixed to the top of the upright which read:

This man is King of the Jews.

Two criminals were executed at the same time.   They were nailed onto crosses erected on either side of Jesus.

The people who walked past added verbal abuse and humiliated him, shouting:

So you are the one who boasted of destroying the temple and rebuilding it in three days.

Get yourself out of this predicament—if you can!

Why don't you get down from the cross yourself?

Let's see how clever you are now!

The chief priest and the scholars added their humiliation.

He healed others and gave them back their lives why can't he heal himself now and take back his own life?

If Jesus is truly God's representative and king of Israel, let him get down from the cross.

If he gets himself down from the cross and we see it, we will believe he is God's representative!—the Messiah!

The two criminals added their abuse.

About midday it turned quite dark and it stayed that way for three hours. Then at the end of that time, Jesus screamed in agony:

Eloi, Eloi, lama sabachthani? (Psalm 22:1)

God—why *do I suffer pain like this?*

God—*you've deserted me—***why?**

Some of the people who were standing at the scene watching said,

He's calling for Elijah!

One ran, picked up a sponge, soaked it in the wine and then put it on the tip of a stick, holding it close to Jesus' mouth, and said:

Perhaps Elijah will come and take him down!

Jesus gave out a loud excruciating cry.

And died!

At that exact moment, the curtain at the entrance to the most sacred part of the temple tore from top to bottom!

The Roman army officer standing in front of the cross who saw Jesus die, remarked:

This man was really very close to God!

Some of the women who were among the close followers of Jesus who had helped him in the Galilee and came with him to Jerusalem, were at the scene including: Mary of Magdala, Mary the mother of the younger James and of Joseph, and Salome.

It was nearly the beginning of the Sabbath, the Jewish sacred day, so Joseph of Arimathea, a highly respected member of the Jewish council, went to Pilate and asked for permission to remove the body from the cross (Joseph was a person who had lived for the day when God would bring in a new world order).

Pilate was surprised at the news that Jesus was dead.   He called in the officer in charge of the execution to check the details.

After the officer had confirmed that Jesus was indeed dead, Pilate gave Joseph permission to remove the body.

Joseph purchased a burial cloth and had Jesus removed from the cross. He wrapped the body and placed it in a rock tomb.   The entrance was closed by a large stone.

Mary of Magdala and Mary the mother of Joseph observed, and noted the location of the tomb.

Postlude: The Empty Tomb

When the sacred day was over, Mary of Magdala, Mary the mother of James, and Salome purchased spices to place in the tomb with the body of Jesus.

At dawn on the Sunday morning they went to the tomb.   On the way they discussed how they would roll the stone away from the entrance.

When they arrived at the place, they saw the huge stone had already been rolled away!

The women entered and were startled to meet a young man dressed in a white robe sitting on the right-hand side of the tomb where the body had been placed.

They became quite frightened.

The man said to them,

Don't be afraid of me!

You are looking for Jesus of Nazareth who was killed!

God has raised him to life!

Hhe has gone from here!

Look, you can see where the body was placed!

Now go and tell the others, especially Peter, Jesus has gone ahead to the Galilee.

You will catch up on him there, just as he told you.

But the women ran away from the tomb.

They were very confused and scared!

They were far too terrified to share their discoveries with anyone else!

Afterword

Mark's gospel has been interpreted in a variety of ways. Sean Kealy has set this out in a succinct and helpful way in *Mark's Gospel: A History of its Interpretation* (1982). His study finishes with 1979. More recent studies are commented on in Adela Yarbro Collins' *The Beginning of the Gospel: Probings of Mark in Context* (1992), especially Chapter One entitled *Is Mark's Gospel a Life of Jesus? The Question of Genre* (pp 1—38).

There is a lively contemporary debate amongst scholars about how an ancient text should be interpreted. This is part of a debate which has been ongoing for at least two and a half centuries. What makes the contemporary debate so interesting is that biblical scholars now work with scholars from other intellectual disciplines in trying to establish the best possible principles for squeezing the last drop of meaning and significance from an ancient text.

An excellent and illuminating book which shows what is possible today is edited by Janice Capel Anderson and Stephen D. Moore and entitled *Mark and Method: New Methods in Biblical Studies* (1992). After an introduction surveying the way *Mark* has been interpreted, five teaching scholars take a particular method and apply it to the gospel to show how it illuminates from a specific angle the meaning of the text. The result is a lively introduction to a range of contemporary ideas about the meaning and significance of *Mark*.

In translating *Mark*, I have found the following studies to be very useful:

David Rhoads and Donald Michie *Mark as Story: An Introduction to the Narrative of a Gospel* (1982). They write:

> 'When we enter the story world of the Gospel of Mark, we enter a world full of conflict and suspense, a world of surprising reversals and strange ironies, a world of riddles and hidden meanings. The hero of the story—perhaps the most memorable in all of literature—is most surprising of all.

> The Gospel of Mark deals with the great issues—life and death,

good and evil, human triumph and human failure. It is not a simple story in which virtue easily triumphs over vice, nor is it a collection of moralisations on life.' (p 1).

I agree! Whoever created this gospel was a brilliant story-teller (Crossan, 1988). Perhaps we need to admit that there may have been more than one person involved in deciding how to shape and use notes taken from spoken sermons about the life of Jesus, references to the Hebrew Bible used to illuminate various points as well as a variety of other sources.

However, in the end, it is more than likely that one person is responsible for creating the storyline and developing it in the way that it appears in this first narrative gospel.

As the reader is drawn into the narrative, the directions of thought change this way and that, often with a subtlety hardly noticed, until the reader is trapped into thinking about what the story means for their own lives, and their own situation.

The ending of the gospel is both abrupt and comes as a surprise. It forces the reader to re-read and rethink the entire story. By the time a reader gets to the end, the presentation has changed so much that it is sometimes difficult to work out if the view one has of the story coincides with the intention of the writer. But if a reader is left puzzled and slightly disturbed and uncomfortable with what has been read or heard, then the creator of the gospel has succeeded in presenting the life of Jesus in they way they intended.

I have deliberately dropped the two endings which later editors have added to bring *Mark*, at that point, into line with *Matthew* and *Luke*.

The confusion and the terror of the women at finding the tomb, where they thought the body of Jesus had been placed, was empty is where the original study concluded. If readers had followed the story-teller to that point, they would be forced to go back to the beginning and re-read the gospel with a new perspective. **Who is this Jesus, whom the story-teller has created?**

The answer to this question is not clear from a first reading of the text or of hearing it read aloud.

A reader or listener is driven back time and time again to re-encounter the figure of Jesus in the text—each time the text is read or heard.

A twentieth century person can never be sure they have picked up and understood everything that is important or even essential for understanding who the Jesus for this gospel is—so far as this writer is concerned!

This gospel is intended to be read or listened to as a whole—at one sitting. To make this as easy as possible, I have dropped from the translation as much of the *church language* as is possible. I have found from classroom experience (University and College level) that most modern translations assume the reader already knows the language the church uses in discussing the identity of Jesus and other related matters. Students have told me otherwise, so I have tried to translate the text as if a twentieth century reader or hearer is encountering *Mark* for the very first time. I have also left out chapter markings and verses to help the flow of language.

I have discovered that the story-teller often introduces stories in an abbreviated fashion that require a reader or hearer to read between the lines and to listen carefully to what is **not being said**, in order to grasp the point being made. Therefore I have occasionally filled out the text to increase its intelligibility for modern readers and listeners.

I think the readers or hearers in the first century setting probably first heard *Mark* read aloud as an entire story. But they would have known more about the figure of Jesus from services of worship and discussions in their local home groups than either the student or the church person of today who seldom discuss the sermons they hear.

However, like my students, they also would have been trying to sort through the issues and to make sense of the life of Jesus as they listened to this gospel being read.

I do not believe at the time *Mark* circulated, the religious language of the Christian community was by any means settled. In fact, I do not think the church as such existed at the time of *Mark* though some steps may have already been taken towards the formation of an organisation in some parts of the Mediterranean world (see Veitch *The Search for Identity and Founding the Church*, 1994).

In the mid seventies, anyone who lived in Israel or was connected by family ties with Israel, would still have been reeling from the effects of the Jewish-Roman war (66–70) with the fall of Masada in (73–74). It would have been a very unsettled time with anger, bitterness and pain just below the surface of people's lives.

The impact of Nero's persecution of *christians* in Rome in 64 would also have taken years to settle.

So those who were this gospel's first readers and hearers would have been far from settled, either in their religious thinking or in their personal and family lives.

The story-teller works out of this context and is influenced by the impact of these events on the lives of all who are caught up in this new religious movement.

The first hearers would have participated in the drama of the story as they listened to it being read. This narrative gospel was the life and thinking of Jesus, told in their situation, in language with which they could identify, using incidents with which they were already familiar. This gospel became very quickly **their** story.

The way the story is constructed reflects the tensions, hopes and fears of those first hearers. The presentation interacts with their own situation and interprets their perceptions of reality with a new set of challenges.

Each part of this gospel interlocks; it is a coherent, well-argued presentation; all the characters fit together into a sequence; the plot and steps leading up to it and away from it, are all carefully thought out by the story-teller. Incidents introduced to heighten tension are deliberately fitted in at particular points. But time and again the story-teller expects the hearers and first readers to be carried along with a deliberate direction of thought and with innuendoes and suggestions that many of the stories enshrine—all deliberately designed to promote further reflection, discussion and debate.

I have found Ched Myers' commentary (1991), though overladen with enormous detail, to be a stimulating interpretation relating this ancient story to our modern situation in the western world.

Myers' commentary uses the text in such a way that the modern reader's own discomfort parallels the discomfort the first hearers and readers must have felt. It is worth reading for the extensive amount of information from studies of life in the first century which Myers has incorporated into his commentary.

A second outstanding study is a major work by Burton Mack, *A Myth of Innocence: Mark and Christian Origins* (1988).

This is a very different piece of work compared to Myers, and interacts with other scholarly studies of *Mark*. It deals with surrounding issues of interpretation and taking us through the layers of the text to encounter a historical Jesus very different from what modern readers think they have encountered when they have heard or read *Mark*.

How then is this gospel to be read today?

I suggest that it should be read as a presentation of the story of Jesus to hearers and readers who were followers of Jesus' way and who met for worship, discussion and friendship in house groups during the early to mid seventies of the **first** century. These people would have been for the most part, second generation followers of the way of Jesus. Some would have still come from a Jewish background, but most would have been non-Jews.

Some forty-five years after the death of Jesus, they were recovering from the traumatic effects of the Jewish-Roman war and its aftermath. The life and thinking of Jesus was created and shaped to meet their needs in this gospel.

Coping with and facing up to death was a major concern of theirs. Some of the cost of following the way of Jesus in the face of tremendous social dislocation, was also another of the issues they had to try and deal with.

Fear, bitterness, hatred, hurt and distrust were essential aspects of the human cost of war and the impact of defeat in social disintegration on the vanquished.

It was almost impossible to be loyal to Jesus in this situation, just as it had been almost impossible to be loyal to Jesus in Rome in the years following Nero's persecution.

It's almost impossible to go on believing in the goodness of God as people experience the death of loved ones in battle or watch them die by crucifixion.

It's almost impossible to believe God is really present in the world in the life of someone who is so cruelly and unjustly treated by other humans.

It is startling to realise that people some forty-five years after Jesus was executed, who were themselves suffering terribly at the hands of the Romans, would have actually begun to deal with their situation and the question of evil, death and suffering, by reading or listening to this presentation of the story of Jesus. But this is surely the situation that we twentieth century readers need to have in mind.

The personal experience of someone in this situation who heard or read this gospel, would have been given a new dimension by this story.

It removed personal tragedies and placed them in a new light as the tragedy of Jesus was explained and interpreted by this superb story-teller.

By externalising the grief, bitterness, hatred, anger and pain, a hero or reader would have been able to take the first faltering steps towards resolving these inner emotions by entering into the spirit of this gospel as it was read to them.

Forgiveness, healing, a sense of wholeness (salvation) is only possible if a person is able to resolve the inner feelings and turmoil caused by such dreadful incidents which come in the guise of war and social disintegration.

So this story of Jesus, created by a story-teller to enable people like the story-teller and others around about to begin to find a way of living a complete human life in spite of all the things that had happened to destroy their confidence and to undermine their belief in the goodness of humankind and in the real presence of God in the world.

War and social disintegration would not only have affected emotions, but also have undermined the intellectual integrity of religious belief.

The story-teller is equal to this issue. Perhaps the story-teller's personal experience with this situation,, enables the story of Jesus to be brilliantly recast, so that belief in God and the goodness of humans is still a possibility.

An obvious conclusion is that living in the way of Jesus is possible, but it involves a demanding moral commitment which marks out the individual and the communities to which they belong and focuses attention on them even more than they have experienced.

If the primary thrust of the gospel is to address the situation of the hearers and readers in the mid seventies, how much of this sermon material edited into the story-teller's presentation is original Jesus of 27–30ce?

The answer to this question varies. According to one group of scholars, only one saying in this gospel can be attributed to Jesus (this is Mark 12: 17, which is about giving to the emperor what belongs to the emperor and giving to God what belongs to God). But there are sixteen others sayings attributed to Jesus, according to this group of scholars, that fall into the category of this *sure sounds like Jesus* (Funk, 1991, p xx— the sayings are set out in full on pp 54 and 55). Two further sayings fall into the ambiguous category of 'maybe' (see pp 55 and 56).

The members of the Jesus seminar who made these judgements are scholars, predominantly engaged in teaching the New Testament in universities and seminaries throughout the United States. Their views are well-researched and informed. This seminar concluded that fifteen percent (or eighteen percent if the *maybe* categories are included) of the sayings attributed to Jesus were uttered by Jesus. Most of the sayings put on the lips of Jesus come from the those who thought deeply about this man and who pieced together a new way of believing in God, based on his life and thought.

So we in the twentieth century do not read this gospel to find out about the Jesus of Galilee who lived until 30ce.

We read it to hear how thinking about the life of Jesus in 75ce allowed the creator of the gospel and the first hearers and readers, grapple with questions about faith in God and the meaning of human life—with the life and thought of *Jesus of Galilee* in mind!

Hearing what they heard and thinking what they thought, we allow the presentation of the life of Jesus in this gospel to interact with our own lives and to prompt and refine the questions we have about faith in God.

Reading the gospel as a whole, recognising the characters in the story and the roles they play as people like us, learning to read between the lines so we can hear the story which was left untold by the editor's snippets woven into the tapestry of the complete presentation, will enable this gospel to impact on our lives and influence our thinking about God.

Belief in God for us in the twentieth century is as difficult as belief in God was for the hearers and readers of this first gospel—although the circumstances for many of us may be different, the problems that we face are almost identical.

We are dominated by scientific humanism which raises fundamental questions about the integrity of belief, in the possibility of believing in the face of the enormous questions which rise out of the suffering, the evil and the social disintegration around us in our modern world.

This situation is little different from that of the hearers of the first century. What is very different is the way they and we grapple with the questions raised for us.

They used thought forms, ideas and stories from their own situation in the first century.

We in the twentieth century have to learn what those stories and ideas meant to them and then find comparable stories and ideas out of our own cultural social situation so we can re-create a story of Jesus, relevant for our times.

But one thing is for certain.

If this gospel finishes where it did, then we are confronted with a Jesus who is not a divine figure but a very human figure. Like the best of us, Jesus struggled with faith in God and at the end may have died with deep disillusionment on his lips. God may have gone on to vindicate his struggle, but that is not clear in the gospel itself. What is a surprise is the way in which this gospel helped to create a centre in faith and belief for the lives of its first hearers and readers.

We might have to read the gospel many times with creative imagination in order to discover this for ourselves.

—Appendix 1—

Two Conclusions to the First Narrative Gospel added some time in the Nineties, soon after the Third Narrative Gospel began to circulate:

—The First Conclusion to the Gospel—

Very early on Sunday after Jesus had risen he appeared first to Mary of Magdala, the woman whose disturbed mind he had healed.

After this meeting, she met up with his companions who were grief-stricken having lost their friend and distraught at having let him down.

In spite of hearing the news that Jesus was alive and that Mary had met with him, they refused to believe it.

Later that day Jesus appeared (in another way) to two of his close friends who were walking out of the city.   Even when these two returned to tell the others of their experience, their story was not taken seriously.

Later still Jesus appeared at mealtime to his eleven companions.   He spoke sternly to them about their unwillingness to believe Mary and the others that he had been raised to life.

He then spoke these words to them:–

> *Go into the whole world and share the good news:* **God is Real! We have experienced God actually present in our own lives and in this world of ours!**

> *Anyone who accepts this as good news and themselves believes God is present in their own lives, and is baptised, will be accepted by God.*

> *Anyone who does not accept this as good news will be condemned.*

All those who accept me as the one who has brought this good news, will do all kinds of marvellous things.

Using my name they will control demons and evil spirits; they will speak new and different languages; they will pick up snakes in their hands without protection; they will even swallow poison and not be violently ill; they will pray and lay hands on the sick who will then get well.

When Jesus had finished speaking, he left his companions and rose into the sky to take his place beside God.

Those to whom Jesus had spoken travelled throughout the world, talking about God being present in the life of Jesus and telling others about everything he had done.

God was with them, and by the example of their lives they showed that what they said was true!

—Appendix 2—

—The Second Ending to the First Gospel—

—these words follow those spoken at the tomb by the young man

The women left quickly and told Peter and the others what had happened to them.

Later on Jesus told his companions to go all over the world, east and west, telling anyone who would listen the sacred and imperishable story of how people could be accepted by God and live forever.

Texts and Versions

Kurt Aland, Matthew Black et al (ed) *The Greek New Testament* UBS 3rd Edition (Corrected) Copyright 1966, 1968, 1975, 1983 United Bible Societies. This is identical to the Nestle-Aland 26th edition. I have used the text on Logos Bible Software with various add-on modules.

Eight Translation New Testament, Tyndale House, Illinois, 1987
    King James Version (AV)
    Living Bible
    Phillips Modern English
    Revised Standard Version (RSV)
    Today's English Version (TEV)
    New International Version (NIV)
    Jerusalem Bible (JB)
    New English Bible (NEB)

Good News Bible, Today's English Version (TEV), American Bible Society, British Edition, 1976.

The Translator's New Testament, The British and Foreign Bible Society, 1973.

The Revised English Bible, Oxford University Press, Oxford, 1989.

The New Revised Standard Version, Oxford University Press, Oxford, 1989.

Bible for Today's Family—New Testament, American Bible Society, New York, 1991.

The Holy Bible, New Century Version, Word Publishing, Dallas, 1991.

Specialist Translations

The New Testament Vol 1, William Barclary, Collins, London, 1968.

The New Testament Vol 2, William Barclary, Collins, London, 1969.

The Other Gospels, Non Canonical Gospel Texts, translated and edited by Ron Cameron, Westminster, Philadelphia, 1982.

The Five Gospels, Robert W. Funk et al, MacMillan Publishing, 1993.

The Gospel of Jesus, (ed) Mgr. Enrico Galbiati, St Paul Publications, Slough, 1979 (original edition 1977 by Instituto S. Gaetano-Vincenza).

The Unvarnished Gospels, Andy Gaus, Threshold books, 1988.

The Complete Gospels, Robert J. Miller (ed) Polebridge Press, Sonoma, 1992.

The Historical New Testament, James Moffatt, T. & T. Clark, Edinburgh, 1901.

The Moffatt Translation of the Bible, James Moffatt, Hodder and Stoughton, London, 1935 (This impression 1987).

The Message: the New Testament in Contemporary English, Eugene H. Peterson, NAV Press, Colorado, 1993.

The Bible in Order (ed) Joseph Rhymer, Darton, Longman and Todd, London, 1975.

The Original New Testament, High J. Schonfield, Firehorn Press, London, (1985).

The Origins of Christianity and the Letters of St Paul, Volume One of the New Testament in a modern Translation and arranged in chronological order, James Veitch, Colcom Press, Red Beach, 1993.

The Search for Identity and Founding the Church, Volume Two of the New Testament in a modern Translation and arranged in chronological order, James Veitch, Colcom Press, Red Beach, 1994.

—Select Bibliography—

Introduction to the New Testament

David L. Barr, *New Testament Story*, Wadsworth, Belmont, 1987.

D.A. Carson, Douglas J. Moo and Len Morris, *An Introduction to the New Testament*, Zandervan, Grand Rapids, 1992.

John Drane, *Introducing the New Testament*, Australian Edition, Albatros Books, Sutherland, 1993.

Howard Clark Kee, *Understanding the New Testament*, Prentice-Hall, New Jersey, 1983.

Helmut Koester, *Introduction to the New Testament*, Volume Two: History in Literature, Fortress Press, Philadelphia, 1982.

W.G. Kummel, *Introduction to the New Testament of Early Christianity*, Fortress Press, Philadelphia, 1982.

Norman Perrin and Dennis C. Duling, *The New Testament: An Introduction*, Harcourt Bruce, New York, 1982.

On Jesus

Richard A. Batty, *Jesus and the Forgotten City*, Baker Bible House, Grand Rapids, 1991.

Marcus J. Borg, *Jesus, A New Vision*, Harper, San Francisco, 1987.

Gunther Bornkamm, *Jesus of Nazareth*, Hodder and Stoughton, London, 1960.

James H. Charlesworth, (ed), *Jesus Jewishness: Exploring the Place of Jesus Within Early Judaism*, Crossroad, New York, 1991.

Gaalyah Cornfeld, (ed), *The Historical Jesus*, Macmillan Publishing Inc., New York, 1982.

John Dominic Crossan, *The Historical Jesus: The Life of Mediterranean Jewish Peasant*, T & T Clark, Edinburgh, 1991.

John Dominic Crossan, *In Parables: The Challenge of the Historical Jesus*, Polebridge Press, Sonoma, 1992.

John Dominic Crossan, *Jesus, A Revolutionary Biography*, Harper Collins, New York, 1993.

Sean Freyne, *Jesus and the Gospels*, Gill and Macmillan, Dublin, 1988.

Robert Funk, *Jesus as Precursor*, (Revised ed by E.F. Beutnee), Polebridge Press, Sonoma, 1993.

Howard Clark Kee, *What Can We Know about JESUS?*, Cambridge University Press, Cambridge, 1990.

Joseph Klausner, *Jesus of Nazareth*, Macmillan Company, New York, 1929.

John Knox, *Jesus, Lord and Christ*, Harper, New York, 1958.

William Manson, *Jesus the Messiah*, Hodder and Stoughton, London, 1943.

John P. Meier, *A Marginal Jew: Rethinking Historical Jesus*, Doubleday, New York, 1991.

Ben F. Meyer, *The Aims of Jesus*, SCM, London, 1979.

Stephen Mitchell, *The Gospel According to Jesus*, Harper Collins, San Francisco, 1991.

Jaroslav Pelikan, *Jesus Through the Centuries*, Yale University Press, New Haven, 1985.

Pheme Perkins, *Jesus as Teacher*, Cambridge University Press, Cambridge, 1990.

John Riches, *The World of Jesus*, Cambridge University Press, 1990.

Daniel Rops, *Jesus in His Time*, Eyre and Spottswoode, London, 1955.

Ellis Rivkin, *What Crucified Jesus?* SCM Press, London, 1984.

E.P. Sanders, *Jesus and Judaism*, Fortress Press, Philadelphia, 1985.

Albert Schweitzer, *The Quest of the Historical Jesus*, A & C Black, London, 1936.

Eduard Schwitzer, *Jesus*, SCM Press, London, 1968.

John Shelby Spong, *Resurrection: Myth or Reality*, Harper Collins, San Francisco, 1994.

John Shelby Spong, *Born of a Woman: A Bishop Reviews the Birth of Jesus*, Harper Collins, San Francisco, 1992.

Graham Stanton, *Jesus of Nazareth in New Testament Preaching*, Cambridge University Press, Cambridge, 1974.

Geza Vermes, *Jesus the Jew*, Fortress Press, Philadelphia, 1973.

Geza Vermes, *The Religion of Jesus the Jew*, SCM, London, 1993.

A.N. Wilson, *Jesus*, Flamingo, London, 1992.

Mark

Janice Capel Anderson and Stephen D. Moore, (eds), *Mark and Method: New Approaches in Biblical Studies*, Fortress Press, Minneapolis, 1992.

Hugh Anderson, *The Gospel of Mark, New Century Bible*, Oliphants, London, 1976.

Adela Yarbo Collins, *The Beginning of the Gospel: Probings of Marcan Content*, Fortress Press, Minneapolis, 1992.

C.E.B. Cranfield, *The Gospel According to St Mark*, Cambridge University Press, 1959.

Leonard Doohan, *Mark: Visiionary of Early Christianity*, Bear & Company, Santa Fe, 1986.

Robert W. Funk, et al, *The Gospel of Mark: Red Letter Edition*, Polbridge Press, Sonoma, 1991.

E.P. Gould, *A Critical and Exegetical Comment on the gospel According to St Mark*, T & T Clark, Edinburgh, 1896.

Morna D. Hooker, *The Son of Man and Mark*, SPCK, London, 1967.

Morna D. Hooker, *A Commentary on the Gospel According to St Mark*, A. & C. Black, London, 1991.

Werner H. Kelber, *Mark's Story of Jesus*, Fortress Press, Philadelphia, 1979.

Sean P. Kealy, *Mark's Gospel: A History of Its Interpretation*, Paulist Press, New York, 1982.

Howard Clark Kee, *Community of the New Age: Studies in Mark's Gospel*, Westminster Press, Philadelphia, 1977.

Koester, Helmut. "History and Development of Mark's Gospel (From Mark to *Secret Mark* and 'Canonical Mark)." In *Colloquy on New Testament Studies: A Time for Reappraisal and Fresh Approaches*, edited by Bruce Corley, 35–57. Proceedings of the Colloquy sponsored and held at Southwestern Baptist Theological Seminary, Fort Worth, Texas, 5–6 November 2980. Macon, GA: Mercer University Press, 1983.

William L. Lane, *The Gospel of Mark*, Marshall, Morgan and Scott, London, 1974.

Burton L. Mack, *A Myth of Innocence: Mark and Christian Origins*, Fortress Press, Philadelphia, 1988.

Ralph Martin, *Mark, Evangelist and Theologian*, Zondervan, Grand Rapids, 1973.

Ched Myers, *Binding the Strong Man: A Political Reading of Mark's Story of Jesus*, Orbis Books, New York, 1991.

David Rhoads and Donald Michie, *Mark a Story: An Introduction to the Narrative of the Gospel*, Fortress Press, Philadelphia, 1982.

Morton Smith, *The Secret Gospel: The Discovery and Interpretations of the Secret Gospel According to Mark*, Yarper and Row, New York, 1973.

Morton Smith, *Clement of Alexandria and a Secret Gospel of Mark*, Harvard University Press, Cambridge (MA), 1973.

Herman C. Waetjen, *A Reordering of Power: A Socio-Political Reading of Mark's Gospel*, Fortress Press, Minneapolis, 1989.

K.S. Wuest, *Mark in the Greek New Testament for the English Reader*, Pickering and Inglis Ltd., London, 1950.

Related Studies

Hendrikus Boers, *Who Was Jesus? The Historical Jesus and the Synoptic Gospels*, Harper, San Francisco, 1989.

John Dominic Crossan, *The Dark Interlude: Towards a Theology of Story*, Polebridge Press, Sonoma, 1988.

John Dominic Crossan, *Four Other Gospels*, Polebridge Press, Sonoma, 1992.

James D.G. Dunne, *The Evidence for Jesus*, SCM, London, 1985.

James D.G. Dunne, *The Parting of the Ways Between Christianity and Judaism: Their Significance For the Character of Christianity*, SCM, London, 1991.

David I. Edwards, *The Real Jesus How Much Can Be Believed?* SCM, London, 1992.

Eusebius, *The History of The Church*, Penguin Classics, London, 1965 (1988).

F.J. Foakes-Jackson, *Josephus and the Jews*, Baker Book House, Grand Rapids, Third Printing, 1981.

Robert W. Funk, *New gospel Parallels*, Vol 1, 2, Polbridge Press, Sonoma, 1990.

Ivan Havener, *Q. The Sayings of Jesus*, Glazier, Wilmington, 1987.

Michael Hilton and Gordon Marshall, *The Gospels and Rabbinic Judaism*, SCM Press, 1988.

Arland D. Jacobson, *The First Gospel: An Introduction to Q,*, Polbridge Press, Sonoma, 1992.

John S. Kloppenborg, et al, *(Q) Thomas Reader*, Polbridge Press, Sonoma, 1990.

Helmut Koester, *Ancient Christian Gospels: Their History and Development,* SCM, London, 1990.

Robin Fox Lane, *Pagans and Christians*, Penguin Books, London, 1986.

Bernard J. Lee, *The Galilean Jewishness of Jesus,* Paulist Press, New York, 1988.

Burton L. Mack, *The Lost Gospel: The Book of Q and Christian Origins,* Harbor, San Francisco, 1983.

Steve Mason, *Josephus and the New Testament*, Hendrickson Peabody, 1993.

John C. Meagher, *Five Gospels: An Account of How the Good News Came to Be*, Winston Press, Minneapolis, 1983.

Ray A. Pritz, *Nazarene, Jewish Christianity,* The Magnes Press, Jerusalem, 1988.

Tessa Rajak, *Josephus: The Historian and His Society*, Fortress Press, Philadelphia, 1983.

Clion L. Rogers, *The Topical Josephus*, Zondervan Publishing House, 1992.

Letty Russell (ed), *Feminists' Interpretations of the Bible*, Blackwell, Oxford, 1988.

E.P. Sanders and Margaret Davies, *Studying the Synoptic Gospels,* SCM, London, 1989.

thomas Sheehan, *The First Coming: How the Kingdom of God Became Christianity*, Random House, New York, 1986.

Graham N. Stanton, *The Gospels and Jesus,* Oxford University Press, Stanton, 1989.

William Whiston, translator, *The Works of Josephus Hendrickson,* Peabody, 1987.

N.T. Wright, *The New Testament and the People of God*, Fortress Press, Minneapolis, 1992.

G.D. Yonge (translator), *The Works of Philo*, Updated Single Volume Edition, Hendrickson Peabody, 1993.

Max Zerwick and Mary Grosvenor, *A Grammatical Analysis of the Greek New Testament* (Unabridged—Fourth Revised Edition), Editrice Pontificio Istituto Biblico, Roma, 1993.

The Author

James Veitch was born in Christchurch and grew up in Oamaru.   After attending Waitaki Boys High School, he went to Otago University where he took a BA in Hebrew.

He then studied for the ministry of the Presbyterian Church at the Theological Hall, Knox College, and completed a BD at the same time. He was the first student to receive the MTh at the University of Otago for a thesis on *Revelation and Old Testament Literature.*   Doctoral studies at the University of Birmingham in England followed.   Under the supervision of Ninian Smart, he prepared a thesis entitled *Christianity, India and the Problem of Revelation: A Contribution to a Theology of Religions.*

In parallel to doctoral studies, he studied at the Selly Oak Colleges in Birmingham, taking courses on various aspects of Islam, Judaism, Primal Religions and Mission History.

Following more than three years in Birmingham, he was appointed to teach Biblical Studies and Asian Religions at the Theological College for Eastern Indonesia in Ujung Pandang, Indonesia.   He served the college as Academic Dean.

After five and a half years in Indonesia, he took up an appointment at Trinity College, Singapore, where he taught Asian Religions, established the Continuing Education degrees for ministers, served as Dean of Students and was involved in supervising advanced doctoral studies under the auspices of the South-East Asian Graduate School of Theology.   He also served for a time as Director for the Institute of the Study of Religion in Society which was then centred at Trinity Theological College.   As a member of the faculty of the Graduate school, he was involved in supervising students in Burma and was able to travel widely in South-East Asia.

In 1978, he took up an appointment in the Religious Studies Department at Victoria University of Wellington.

James Veitch is actively involved in the life of the Christian community and in facilitating contacts and understanding between peoples of different faiths.